A Darker Shade of Dodger Blue the McCourt Era

Allen Schery

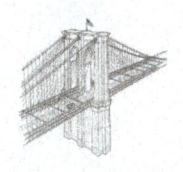

Brooklyn Bridge Books

Copyright © 2025 by Allen Schery

All rights reserved.

No portion of this book may be reproduced in any form without written permission from the publisher or author, except as permitted by U.S. copyright law.

Contents

1. A Boston Dream   1
2. The Deal   10
3. A Fractured Fanbase   15
4. On-Field Performance   20
5. The Real Estate Play   26
6. Growing Discontent   37
7. The Divorce   47
8. MLB Intervention   54
9. The Sale   62
10. A New Era   72
11. Aftermath   82
12. The McCourt Legacy   94

Bibliography   109

Endnotes   126

Chapter 1

A Boston Dream

Frank McCourt's ambition, a force that would eventually propel him from Boston's intricate real estate landscape to the sun-drenched glare of Los Angeles baseball, was deeply rooted in his upbringing and the city that shaped him. Born into a prominent Boston family with deep ties to civic and sporting life, McCourt inherited a passion for the game and an almost ancestral yearning for ownership. This desire transcended mere fandom to become a profound psychological imperative: it was not simply about possessing a team, but about embodying a civic identity, wielding a cultural scepter, and—perhaps most crucially—achieving immortality through association with an institution larger than any individual.

While his early life wasn't marked by overt hardship, it instilled in him a keen understanding of leverage and opportunity—a pragmatic worldview honed amid Boston's competitive real estate market. The urban environment of Boston, with its layered history of political maneuvering and economic transformation, served as a crucible for his developing entrepreneurial spirit, teaching him that actual influence often lay in the strategic acquisition and manipulation of tangible assets.

The Real Estate Crucible

His initial forays into real estate were characterized by audacious vision and a willingness to navigate the often-murky waters of urban development. From residential conversions in established neighborhoods to acquiring and revitalizing distressed commercial properties, McCourt honed his instincts for market cycles and zoning complexities. His early successes were built upon identifying undervalued properties and orchestrating complex financial arrangements to unlock their latent potential. He was a master of the long game, understanding that patience, aggressive negotiation, and a keen eye for legislative loopholes could yield immense returns.

One of his most significant undertakings—arguably the most illustrative of his operational philosophy—was his involvement in transforming Boston's Seaport District. This ambitious project, aimed at revitalizing a sprawling industrial waterfront into a vibrant commercial and residential hub, showcased McCourt's capacity for large-scale development. However, it also highlighted certain aspects of his approach that would later draw scrutiny.

Critics often pointed to his adeptness at securing substantial public subsidies and tax abatements, arguing that these incentives, while ostensibly designed to spur economic growth, disproportionately benefited private developers like McCourt. The mechanisms for these subsidies often involved intricate political lobbying and the cultivation of relationships with key municipal figures, allowing McCourt's ventures to receive preferential treatment in a highly competitive market.

The use of eminent domain—a powerful governmental tool enabling the acquisition of private property for public use—was another contentious point. Some suggested that its application in specific McCourt-affiliated projects blurred the lines between public good and private gain. Small businesses or long-standing residents might find their properties targeted for acquisition, ostensibly for public infrastructure, only for the land to be subsequently transferred to private developers for commercial projects.

While legally permissible, the ethical implications of such maneuvers, particularly when they displaced established communities for large-scale corporate development, were frequently debated. These practices painted a picture of a developer who was exceptionally skilled at leveraging political connections and public resources to advance his private interests—a characteristic that would echo in his later stewardship of the Dodgers.

The Psychology of Power

The psychological drive behind McCourt's relentless pursuit of wealth and influence was complex, likely stemming from a deep-seated need for validation and control. For many entrepreneurs, the accumulation of capital is not merely an end in itself but a means to an even grander objective: the acquisition of power and status that transcends mere financial success. For McCourt, this ultimate objective manifested as the ownership of a major sports franchise.

It was a dream that had simmered for decades, a personal grail that symbolized the pinnacle of achievement in a city where sports heroes were revered almost as deities. The Red Sox, in particular, held mythical status, embodying the collective hopes and frustrations of generations of Bostonians. To own such an entity was to become a custodian of history, a figure of immense public visibility, and a participant in a narrative far grander than any real estate deal.

This aspiration was not simply a logical extension of his business acumen; it was an emotional and psychological imperative, a quest for a form of legacy that money alone could not buy. The allure of the ballpark, the roar of the crowd, the visceral connection to a community through shared triumphs and defeats—these were the intangible assets that McCourt truly coveted, believing that they offered a deeper, more resonant form of success than any balance sheet could reflect.

This yearning for control extended beyond mere financial dominion; it was a desire to shape narratives, influence public sentiment, and command a sphere of influence that transcended the transactional nature of his real estate empire. The psychological satisfaction derived from being at the helm of a beloved institution, a focal point of civic pride, offered a form of validation that the quiet accumulation of property could not.

The Red Sox Pursuit

His repeated, albeit ultimately unsuccessful, attempts to acquire the Boston Red Sox, spanning over two decades, were formative experiences, shaping his understanding of the intricate dance between sports, finance, and public perception. While undoubtedly frustrating, each failed bid served as a masterclass in the complexities of sports ownership, revealing the unique blend of business acumen, political savvy, and public relations dexterity required to navigate such a high-profile acquisition.

He learned the nuances of league approval processes, the delicate art of valuing a cultural institution, and the immense power of fan sentiment. These lessons, absorbed through the crucible of disappointment, refined his strategy and sharpened his resolve. The psychological resilience required to pursue such a monumental goal repeatedly, despite setbacks, speaks to a profound inner conviction—a belief in his destiny to command a major league team.

It was a testament to a personality that viewed obstacles not as deterrents but as challenges to be meticulously overcome, a characteristic that would later prove both his strength and, ultimately, his undoing. The public nature of these failed bids often played out in the Boston media, serving as an early exposure to the intense scrutiny accompanying sports ownership—a preview of the relentless spotlight that would later illuminate every facet of his life and business dealings in Los Angeles.

The American Dream Reconsidered

The philosophical dimension of McCourt's ambition can be viewed through the lens of the American Dream, albeit a version filtered through the prism of late 20th- and early 21st-century capitalism. It was a dream not merely of upward mobility but of transcending one's origins to become a titan—a figure whose influence extended beyond the confines of mere commerce into the realm of cultural significance.

For McCourt, owning a sports team was the ultimate expression of this transcendence, a public declaration of arrival at the apex of power and influence. It was a pursuit of a legacy that would endure beyond the transient nature of real estate deals, a desire to etch his name into the annals of sporting history. This yearning for a lasting imprint, for a form of immortality through association with an iconic institution, speaks to a fundamental human desire to leave a mark and imbue one's life with purpose beyond personal accumulation.

However, this ambition, while powerful, also carried within it the seeds of its potential destruction. The very public nature of sports ownership would expose his methods and motivations to an unprecedented level of scrutiny—a level far beyond anything he had encountered in the comparatively private world of real estate development. The ethical compromises and strategic leveraging of public resources that had served him well in Boston's development scene would find a far less forgiving audience in the emotionally charged arena of professional sports, where the team was often seen as a public trust rather than a private asset.

The Westward Turn

As opportunities in Boston for acquiring a major sports franchise proved elusive, McCourt's gaze began to drift westward, drawn by the allure of new possibilities and, perhaps, a less entrenched establishment. The psychological shift from a deeply personal, almost tribal, desire to own the Red Sox to a more pragmatic, yet still deeply ambitious, pursuit of the Los Angeles Dodgers marked a pivotal moment.

It was a recognition that the essence of his dream—the ownership of a major league baseball team—could be realized elsewhere, even if the emotional connection was not as deeply ingrained as it was with his hometown club. This transition underscored his adaptability and unwavering commitment to his ultimate goal, demonstrating that while the specific object of his desire might change, the underlying drive remained constant.

The stage was set not in the familiar brick and ivy of Fenway but under Southern California's expansive skies, where a different kind of legacy awaited its architect. The journey from Boston's tightly knit real estate circles to the sprawling, celebrity-infused landscape of Los Angeles was more than a geographical relocation; it was a profound psychological and professional metamorphosis, preparing him for a challenge that would test the very limits of his ambition and his capacity for control.

Chapter 2
The Deal

Frank McCourt's acquisition of the Los Angeles Dodgers unfolded like a high-stakes drama in which the boundary between boardroom calculation and baseball romance blurred into one audacious act. Across the diamond of Chavez Ravine, McCourt saw not only the echo of cheers but also the promise of transforming acres of asphalt and grass into a grander vision. His approach was rooted in the belief that baseball and real estate were two sides of the same coin—one fueled by passion, the other by cold, hard capital.

When Rupert Murdoch's News Corporation decided to sell the Dodgers in 2003, it was with the detached efficiency of a ship's captain abandoning a weary vessel. Murdoch had paid $311 million in 1998 for the franchise, lured by the promise of steady regional broadcasting revenue for Fox Sports Net West. Yet rising player salaries, the complexities of running a lone team within a sprawling media empire, and shifting corporate priorities had turned Dodger Blue into a fiscal liability. Over six seasons, News Corp. reportedly bled $165 million—a sum rivaling the cost of signing a marquee player. In polished boardrooms under glass-and-steel ceilings, the Dodgers ceased to be a cultural beacon and became a line item to offload, a casualty of shifting strategic imperatives.

Frank McCourt arrived with the energy of a man who had spent years dreaming by Fenway Park, only to discover his dream awaiting him on the West Coast. His Boston accent cut through the LA air as he described Dodger Stadium not merely as hallowed grounds but as the centerpiece of a sprawling real estate portfolio. He painted vivid pictures of retail promenades nestled among orange groves, luxury condominiums overlooking the diamond's green expanse, and entertainment districts humming with life. For McCourt, each ticket sold and each hot dog devoured was a footstep toward a larger destiny—one where the roar of the crowd blended with the hum of construction to rewrite the story of Chavez Ravine.

When he made his bid of approximately $430 million for the Dodgers, the stadium, and adjacent land, observers were stunned not by the price tag but by the structure of the deal. McCourt did something almost unheard of in sports: he leveraged the seller's own resources. News Corp. agreed to loan him roughly $196 million, smoothing their tax obligations while financing their own exit, and Bank of America supplied the remaining $225 million, backed by McCourt's parking-lot empire in Boston. In practical terms, McCourt touched none of his own cash to secure the transaction. Instead, he wove together layers of debt like a master tailor stitching a bespoke suit—each loan serving as both fabric and seam. The resulting arrangement was so elegant in its financial choreography that it shimmered with promise even as it planted seeds of future fragility.

On the first night after the sale, fans gathered outside Dodger Stadium under California stars, clutching foam fingers and relics from the O'Malley era. Some cheered the arrival of a passionate owner; others whispered warily, recalling the corporate coldness of News Corp. Billboard-sized posters proclaimed "Welcome, Frank!" while casual conversations floated rumors of luxury condos sprouting where parking lots once lay. Season-ticket holders—many of whom had sat in the same seat for decades—wondered whether their cherished views of the field would soon be shadowed by cranes. Yet beneath the surface skepticism lay a flicker of hope: that this new proprietor would breathe life into the team, investing in both players and the community that had long loved them.

Major League Baseball's approval process, overseen by Commissioner Bud Selig, required a delicate blend of financial vetting and political diplomacy. League insiders later admitted that McCourt's debt-laden structure raised eyebrows—few teams should hinge entirely on loans secured against distant parking lots. Yet in the end, the sale was green-lit, signaling that baseball was changing. Gone were the days when ownership passed solely among storied families; now a developer with no upfront cash could claim the throne. By endorsing the deal, MLB embraced a new paradigm in which balance sheets and leverage ratios mattered almost as much as batting averages and ERA.

When the keys to the stadium were handed over in early 2004, McCourt stood beneath the stadium lights in a Dodger-blue tie, his breath visible in the crisp evening air. He spoke of renewal, of restoring Dodger Stadium to its former glory, of building a legacy that would endure longer than any scoreboard. The crowd applauded, but beneath the hopeful claps lay an unspoken question: could a team, a community treasure, truly flourish under such intricate financial engineering?

In the months that followed, McCourt's hands-on presence—inspecting construction sites, greeting fans in the parking lots, and attending spring training with the ease of an old friend—suggested that his heart was as invested as his balance sheet. Yet the towering structures of debt remained, invisible to most, casting long shadows over every promise he made. From the outset, every home run and every refinancing would be intertwined, the bright lights of Major League Baseball illuminating not only the players on the field but also the precarious ledger lines that underpinned the fate of a beloved franchise.

Chapter 3
A Fractured Fanbase

Frank McCourt's arrival in Chavez Ravine in early 2004 was heralded as a breath of fresh air for Dodgers fans long weary of corporate indifference. With his Boston accent cutting through the Southern California air and an almost evangelistic fervor, he vowed to restore the franchise to its former glory. In ballpark speeches warmed by floodlights and on radio waves carrying his promise, he spoke of being a "hands-on" owner, personally committed to signing star talent and transforming the fan experience at Dodger Stadium. He painted vivid scenes of family festivals on the outfield grass, open-air concerts beneath the night sky, and concession stands offering everything from gourmet tacos to craft beer—a far cry from the stale hot dogs and plastic seats of recent years.

Psychologically, McCourt faced the monumental task of stepping into shoes fashioned by the O'Malley family's almost paternal stewardship. He craved that same reverence, striving to present himself as a benevolent custodian rather than a calculating entrepreneur. Early public appearances alongside his then-wife Jamie reinforced the image of a family united in service of the team, sharing laughter with season-ticket holders and posing for photos with wide-eyed children. Yet beneath the handcrafted pleasantries lurked the inescapable reality of the massive debt underpinning his purchase—a reality that often surfaced in ill-timed strategic shifts and public relations stumbles.

Almost immediately, McCourt's obsession with the real estate potential of Chavez Ravine collided with baseball tradition. Where veterans saw turf and dugouts, he saw vast parking lots ripe for retail complexes and high-rise condominiums. Concourse renovations brightened dim corridors; repainted seating sections glowed in fresh Dodger blue. New food vendors introduced artisanal popcorn and vegan sliders, delighting casual fans even as purists scoffed at distractions from the game itself. Rumors spread of a Dodger Hall of Fame and Museum—an ambitious project championed, designed and curated by Allen Schery, already had 250,000 Dodger artifacts collected. Allen was handpicked from Cooperstown by Tommy Hawkins to curate and craft interactive exhibits tracing the Dodgers' rich lineage. Schery envisioned life-size recreations of the Dodgers former fields and windows on Dodger History and audio kiosks playing Vin Scully's timeless calls, turning the cavernous underbelly of the stadium into a bustling cultural hub. Yet despite completed designs and community presentations brimming with enthusiasm, McCourt's museum dream remained on paper—its unbuilt walls a poignant reminder of promises eclipsed by financial imperatives. He claimed it was on his radar but nobody could find the radar.

Behind closed doors, McCourt's swift consolidation of power unsettled the front-office executives who had operated with relative autonomy under News Corp. Gone were the days of distant oversight; now every decision—from clubhouse staffing to stadium branding—bore the unmistakable stamp of the owner's vision. His son Drew spearheaded a new dynamic pricing model, reclassifying long-standing seats as "premium" based on opponent popularity. Overnight, loyal holders in the left-field pavilion awoke to doubled ticket prices. Fans who had rooted for generations felt their devotion commodified by opaque algorithms, sparking outrage that rippled through online forums and local talk radio.

Small acts intended to endear only deepened the rift: the much-ballyhooed "Twelve-Dollar Giveaway" distributed cheap plastic megaphones and poorly printed tote bags, tokens that many scoffed at as penny-wise public relations. Meanwhile, whispers circulated in clubhouse corridors and sports bars about McCourt's opulent personal spending—luxury cars, out-of-town vacations, and private jet charters—juxtaposed against reported budget constraints on player payroll. When future Hall of Famer Adrián Beltré, fresh off a career-best 48-homer season, departed for Seattle rather than accept a modest contract extension, the message was unmistakable: financial pragmatism trumped competitive ambition.

On Opening Day, the sun shone bright over Chavez Ravine as veterans tipped their caps and rookies took tentative looks at the stands. The crowd cheered McCourt's ceremonial first pitch, but beneath the roar lay a simmering question: could this man, whose heart seemed invested in property valuations as much as batting averages, truly honor the soul of a storied franchise? As fans streamed home under streetlights, conversations shifted from optimism to wary skepticism. The promise of a revitalized ballpark and star-studded roster had given way to suspicion that the Dodgers were becoming collateral in a real estate empire.

Even as spring training unfolded under palm-lined skylines, McCourt's visible presence—patrolling the parking lots in a Dodger-blue windbreaker, chatting up vendors at concession stands—belied the mounting tension within the organization. Coaches found their roster-building strategies superseded by financial memos; scouts received notices to prioritize cost-controlled talents over high-priced free agents. The underlying duality of McCourt's mission—to marry baseball glory with property development—reverberated through every department, fracturing the once-unified culture. Where once the front office rallied around a shared dream of pennants, now meetings often turned into debates over debt service and land-use permits. The early days in Chavez Ravine, rather than cementing a new era of prosperity and genuine fan connection, inadvertently laid the groundwork for deep mistrust and acrimony, setting the stage for the tumultuous seasons to come.

Chapter 4
On-Field Performance

Frank McCourt's tenure at the helm of the Dodgers produced one of the most dramatic eras in Chavez Ravine's storied history, a time when the thrill of unexpected triumphs clashed with the unsettling hum of financial unease. The story began in 2004 under manager Jim Tracy, when a team infused with veteran grit—Cesar Izturis's slick shortstop play, Steve Finley's veteran steadiness, Paul Lo Duca's fiery energy behind the plate—and young firebrands like Adrian Beltré electrified the ballpark. Beltré's career-best 48 homers became the stuff of legend, each swing painting night skies over the palm trees with echoes of possibility. Dodgers fans, clutching rally towels and foam fingers, ignited the stands, sending the team to a 93-win season and the NL West crown. Yet the bitter irony of that breakthrough lay in its aftermath: Beltré, whose name had become synonymous with Chavez Ravine's renaissance, walked away that winter to Seattle, a casualty of McCourt's stringent payroll philosophy.

The following seasons unfolded like a novel in which characters constantly shifted roles. In 2005, McCourt recruited Paul DePodesta, the statistical savant whose "Moneyball" methods upended baseball orthodoxy in Oakland. DePodesta's analytical charts and rigorous cost-benefit projections clashed with Tracy's clubhouse camaraderie; veterans like Eric Karros found themselves grappling with lineup decisions driven by metrics rather than gut instinct. The result was confusion on the field and a disappointing 71-91 record that tested fans' faith. Yet even in that slump, sparks of promise flickered: rookie pitchers like Chad Billingsley flashed arm strength, and glimpses of future stars hinted at a farm system that McCourt's front office had quietly nurtured.

By 2006, Grady Little arrived, bringing the patient wisdom of Fenway Park to Los Angeles. Under Little, the Dodgers rediscovered a sense of unity. Russell Martin emerged as a defensive stalwart and offensive catalyst, while Nomar Garciaparra—another transplant from McCourt's unfulfilled Red Sox dreams—found his groove at first base. The team rallied late in the season, charging to an 88-74 record and a Wild Card berth. Fans roared their approval as Little's easygoing style coaxed timely hits and late-inning heroics, yet the perennial question lingered: would McCourt's checkbook keep pace with championship aspirations?

The arrival of Joe Torre in 2008 felt like destiny. Torre, whose résumé glittered with World Series rings from New York, brought an aura of calm authority. His first season saw an earthquake of excitement when the blockbuster acquisition of Manny Ramirez turned Chavez Ravine into "Mannywood." Ramirez's every swing unleashed seismic cheers that rattled the stadium foundations; his larger-than-life personality and clutch homers transformed routine games into must-see events. Fans decked themselves in No. 99 jerseys, vendors sold out of Ramirez bobbleheads within minutes, and local radio airwaves buzzed with debate over his on- and off-field antics. Under Torre's gentle guidance, the Dodgers captured back-to-back NL West titles and reached consecutive NLCS showdowns. Their march to October was fueled by a potent blend of veteran savvy—Derek Lowe's steady right arm, Jeff Kent's clutch hitting—and the blossoming brilliance of homegrown stars: Matt Kemp's highlight-reel catches, Andre Ethier's consistent on-base prowess, and Clayton Kershaw's flamethrower fastball that hinted at a generational ace in the making.

Yet even amid these heady highs, shadows lingered. Boardroom whispers spoke of looming debt payments; architects surveyed Dodger Stadium's parking lots for future developments even as fans sung "Take Me Out to the Ball Game." Every Mannywood promotion, every sold-out concession stand, became fodder for financial spreadsheets rather than payroll expansions. When Ramirez re-signed for two years and $45 million after 2008, it felt like a late-season fireworks show—dazzling but ephemeral, not the start of a sustained spending campaign.

As Kershaw matured into a dominant force—his curveball carving hitters like carved wood—the team's nucleus strengthened. Kemp sprinted into MVP conversations, his joyous smile on the basepaths capturing the city's imagination. Ethier's late-inning pinch hits became narrative gold in local tabloids. Yet for every roar of approval, there was an undercurrent of unease: ticket prices climbed under dynamic pricing algorithms; luxury suite discussions overshadowed free-agent rumors; talk show hosts contrasted Ramirez's promotion-driven contract with Beltré's neglected extension.

When Torre retired after 2010, Don Mattingly stepped into the dugout in 2011 with a groundswell of goodwill. "Donnie Baseball," as he was affectionately known, infused the clubhouse with warmth, mentoring rookies like Dee Gordon and chiding veteran sluggers to embrace team over self. But off the field, McCourt's personal life splintered into public spectacle. Divorce filings made headlines; reports emerged of unpaid vendors and MLB warnings. The mood at spring training soured as lawyers replaced coaches in headlines. Mattingly's players—Kershaw, Kemp, Kenley Jansen in the bullpen—wore expressions of frustration even as they battled admirably on the field. The team stumbled to a sub-.500 record, their on-field struggles amplified by the cacophony of off-field chaos.

Through it all, Chavez Ravine's palm trees bore silent witness to a franchise suspended between exhilarating near-misses and heartbreaking financial realities. Fans continued to drive through Sunset Boulevard traffic, clutching programs and foam fingers, refusing to let boardroom memos dictate their devotion. Walk-off singles and diving catches remained sacred moments, etched into the Blu Fisher parking lot walls in graffiti and banners. Yet each celebration, each late-inning hero, carried a hint of fragility—an awareness that the quartet of wins and losses was inextricably bound to balance-sheet footnotes far from the roar of the crowd.

McCourt's era, in retrospect, stands as a testament to both the power and peril of modern sports ownership. It showcased homegrown talent's resilience—Kershaw's Cy Young seasons, Kemp's MVP-caliber runs, Ethier's consistency—but also highlighted how financial architecture can uplift or undermine a team's spirit. The philosophical debate it sparked endures: can a franchise honor its cultural and civic legacy while also serving as a linchpin in an owner's sprawling financial empire? The answer, as witnessed under Chavez Ravine's stadium lights, was neither simple nor conclusive. Instead, it breathed in the crack of bats, the squeal of cleats, and the restless pulse of a fanbase that, regardless of financial storms, never stopped believing in the Dodgers' greatness.

Chapter 5
The Real Estate Play

Frank McCourt's acquisition of the Los Angeles Dodgers was, at its core, a masterclass in financial engineering —a real estate play disguised as a passionate pursuit of a beloved sports franchise. His vision for the team extended far beyond the ninety feet between bases or the dimensions of the outfield fence; it encompassed the vast, valuable acreage of Chavez Ravine, which he shrewdly perceived as a largely untapped goldmine of potential development. The philosophical underpinning of his ownership was deeply rooted in leveraging tangible assets to generate massive amounts of capital, a strategy meticulously honed over decades in the fiercely competitive Boston real estate market. He saw the Dodgers not merely as a baseball club with a storied past and a loyal following but as the quintessential centerpiece of a sprawling, multi-faceted enterprise. To facilitate this ambitious vision, he meticulously crafted an intricate, often bewildering web of corporate entities. These structures were expressly designed to maximize financial liquidity and enable complex debt financing. Frequently, it would later be revealed, at the expense of transparency, the team's finances, and ultimately, the baseball club's operational health and competitive viability. Early reports by financial experts and local media, like the Los Angeles Times, subtly hinted at the high leverage involved in his acquisition, raising initial questions about its long-term stability.

The deliberate separation and subsequent strategic leveraging of the Dodger Stadium parking lots were central to McCourt's overarching strategy. These vast tracts of land, encompassing hundreds of acres, had traditionally been seen by previous ownerships and the public alike as mere functional adjuncts to the ballpark, essential for game-day operations but not as independent profit centers. However, in McCourt's estimation, these were prime pieces of undeveloped or underdeveloped urban real estate, possessing immense, unrealized development potential. Almost immediately upon acquiring the team, he meticulously carved out these parking lots into a separate corporate entity, Chavez Ravine Properties LLC, effectively and legally divorcing the most valuable physical asset from the baseball club itself, which remained primarily under the control of Dodger Holdings LLC. This corporate maneuver was not merely an accounting formality or a simple structural adjustment; it was, in retrospect, a foundational and profoundly strategic element of his entire financial architecture. The parking lots, now legally separated and largely free from the encumbrances of the baseball team's operational costs, player salaries, and contractual obligations, could then be independently mortgaged and leveraged for massive, multi-million-dollar loans. This crucial strategy allowed McCourt to extract significant capital from these valuable, tangible assets, often to service his substantial debts incurred from the acquisition—reportedly a $150 million loan from News Corp. and a $175 million line of credit from Bank of America—or inject much-needed liquidity into his other ventures, including his increasingly public and lavish personal lifestyle. The philosophical implication of this financial separation was profound: it treated a vital, integrated part of what many considered a public institution and cultural landmark as a detached, purely private commodity to be exploited for maximum individual financial gain rather than serving the holistic needs and long-term stability of the overall franchise. This fundamental redefinition of the Dodgers' assets laid the insidious groundwork for the complex, intertwined financial structures that would later become a source of intense scrutiny, legal contention, and widespread public outrage, foreshadowing potential claims related to the team's ability to meet its financial obligations to Major League Baseball.

The financial structures McCourt put in place were remarkably complex and often opaque, a testament to his acumen as a financier and his willingness to push the boundaries of corporate finance; however, they were also deeply problematic due to their inherent lack of transparency and pervasive conflicts of interest. The initial acquisition, famously conducted with "not a penny" of his cash, was enabled by a substantial loan from News Corp. and a significant line of credit from Bank of America. This initial layer of debt was then systematically compounded by numerous refinancing efforts, additional loans from various financial institutions, and intricate inter-company transfers, often secured by the very assets that were part of his convoluted corporate empire. The multiple corporations he established—a sprawling network that included not just Dodger Holdings LLC and Chavez Ravine Properties LLC but various other limited liability companies (LLCs) often bearing names like Dodger Baseball LLC or Dodger Stadium TopCo LLC, all operating under the broader umbrella of The McCourt Group—were not simply for organizational clarity. They were meticulously crafted to facilitate a constant, often dizzying, flow of funds between entities, primarily through what are known as "related-party transactions," where one McCourt-controlled entity would ostensibly lend money to another McCourt-controlled entity, often at terms favorable to the lender. For instance, Dodger Holdings LLC, which owned the baseball team, would pay substantial "rent" or "lease payments"—sometimes reported to be in the tens of millions annually—to Chavez Ravine Properties LLC for using the parking lots—effectively paying another McCourt entity for assets integral to the team's operations. Jamie McCourt, as CEO, was also privy to and involved in the intricate financial decisions and inter-company transactions that defined this structure. These elaborate inter-company transactions, while potentially offering significant tax advantages and creating an illusion of robust economic activity, also generated a highly opaque system where it became exceedingly difficult for outside observers, including Major League Baseball itself, to trace the ultimate destination of funds accurately and to independently assess the proper financial health and operational viability of the baseball club in isolation. Critics and later investigators, including the Commissioner's office, would vociferously argue that these intricate structures allowed McCourt to extract vast sums of cash from the Dodgers organization, ostensibly as "management fees" (often calculated as a percentage of revenue, further incentivizing short-term revenue over long-term investment) or "repayments" for "loans" to other parts of his burgeoning empire, effectively using the iconic baseball team as a highly liquid personal ATM.

Utilizing these complex corporate structures frequently involved what critics and later league investigators would deem "specious claims" and highly questionable accounting practices designed to obscure the actual financial state of the franchise. McCourt's various entities would sometimes report substantial "profits" on paper, often derived from these inter-company transactions, including the sale of development rights related to the stadium land or the refinancing of debt, which appeared as "revenue" in specific ledgers. However, these reported profits rarely, if ever, translated into increased direct investment in the actual baseball team's operational budget or significant upgrades to its aging infrastructure beyond superficial stadium improvements. Instead, the actual operational cash flow generated by the Dodgers seemed to vanish into the labyrinthine corporate structure, ostensibly to service the growing mountain of debt he had accumulated, to fund other McCourt ventures, or to support his increasingly ostentatious personal lifestyle. The philosophical debate centers critically on corporate ethics, transparency, and accountability: How can an owner treat a public trust, such as a professional sports team, as a purely private financial instrument, shielded by layers of corporate complexity and dubious accounting?

The "miserliness" that became a defining characteristic of McCourt's ownership, deeply frustrating the fan base, was thus not merely a general reluctance to spend on players, but a direct, systemic consequence of this intricate financial engineering. The cash that could have been readily used to retain beloved star players, invest in deeper roster talent, or significantly upgrade the fundamentally aging Dodger Stadium infrastructure was instead systematically diverted to service the massive debt load he had accumulated or to flow into other, less scrutinized, parts of his multi-faceted empire. It created a profound operational inefficiency for the baseball club, as the team continually struggled to compete on an equal financial footing with rivals with more straightforward and financially robust ownership structures, consistently hampered by an inability to access the capital it generated.

Further exacerbating the operational inefficiencies and directly contributing to the perception of a financially strained and poorly managed organization was the widely perceived and often criticized inefficiency of Drew McCourt, the son of the McCourts, who was installed in a high-ranking executive position overseeing significant business operations, including ticketing and marketing. While Frank McCourt's philosophical approach was often one of absolute trust and strategic empowerment for his inner circle, particularly family members, this high-profile nepotistic appointment proved to be a significant detriment to the organization's public image and operational effectiveness. Drew McCourt's direct responsibility for the deeply controversial dynamic pricing model and the problematic, widespread reclassification of seating sections, which notoriously alienated and infuriated legions of long-time season ticket holders, demonstrated a fundamental disconnect with the core fanbase and a conspicuous lack of seasoned experience in managing a large-scale, public-facing enterprise with such high emotional stakes. Beyond just the ticketing fiascos, there were pervasive perceptions of broader inefficiencies in marketing strategies, the aggressive pursuit of revenue generation (beyond the leveraging of real estate), and the general day-to-day business management of the numerous corporate entities under his purview. These inefficiencies created significant internal friction, contributed to missed revenue opportunities, and amplified external criticism, often resulting in direct financial shortfalls for the baseball club. The psychological impact of this apparent managerial ineptitude was considerable: it reinforced the increasingly prevalent idea that the Dodgers' front office was not being run by seasoned baseball or business professionals guided by merit but rather by individuals whose familial loyalty superseded their actual competence, further contributing to the financial strain on the team. It, in turn, directly impacted the critical operational budget available for baseball operations, providing another tangible link in the narrative of "miserliness" driven by what was perceived as mismanagement and the owner's intertwined personal and familial priorities.

The intricate web of corporations and sophisticated financial maneuvers McCourt meticulously established—from carving out the parking lots into separate LLCs to the numerous inter-company loans, convoluted lease agreements, and substantial "management fees"—created a systemic structure that was legally complex but ethically fraught from the perspective of public trust and sound business governance for a sports franchise. It allowed him to utilize the Dodgers' vast assets and the substantial revenue the team generated as primary collateral and a continuous source of cash flow for his broader, highly leveraged financial empire, often blurring the lines between personal wealth, corporate debt, and team finances in ways unprecedented in baseball. The philosophical implications of this approach were far-reaching and deeply unsettling for many:

It fundamentally challenged the traditional understanding of sports ownership as a blend of astute business acumen and profound public stewardship, pushing it firmly into the realm of pure financial asset stripping and speculative real estate development. The "specious claims" were not always outright, provable falsehoods but rather highly selective interpretations of financial data, strategically designed to present a public picture of solvency, robust profitability, and imminent investment that starkly belied the underlying mountain of debt and the continuous extraction of funds from the Dodgers organization. This pervasive lack of transparency, coupled with the complex financial dealings, generated profound distrust and frustration within the league, among the media, and, most importantly, among the loyal fan base. The psychological consequence was a profound and irreparable erosion of trust. Fans, in particular, felt a deep sense of betrayal, believing that the iconic team, which they viewed as their community's pride and a sacred civic institution, was being callously manipulated and systematically drained for the owner's gain rather than being nurtured and invested in for competitive success. This complex financial architecture, meticulously designed for McCourt's benefit and to circumvent traditional baseball financing models, ultimately proved unsustainable and catastrophically fragile, leading to the highly publicized disputes with Major League Baseball, culminating in intervention and legal battles, and inexorably setting the stage for the dramatic and humiliating unraveling of his ownership, unequivocally demonstrating that a purely financial philosophy, when divorced from the essential public trust inherent in sports, was ultimately untenable and prone to disastrous consequences. Indeed, the eventual bankruptcy filing of the Dodgers would serve as the ultimate legal and financial indictment of this unsustainable model.

Chapter 6
Growing Discontent

The initial cautious optimism that greeted Frank McCourt's arrival in Chavez Ravine, already frayed by early missteps in ticketing and the perceived parsimony in player retention, gradually metastasized into a pervasive and deeply rooted discontent among the Dodgers' faithful. This growing dissatisfaction was not merely a reaction to intermittent on-field performance; it stemmed from an increasingly public and unsettling scrutiny of the team's finances and McCourt's personal spending, fostering a profound sense of betrayal from perceived dishonesty and deception. Initially subtle, the early signs of financial strain began to manifest with alarming frequency, revealing the inherent fragility of the highly leveraged acquisition model and the true, often obscured, cost of his complex corporate architecture. This period marked a pivotal shift, as the initial veneer of a passionate, hands-on owner began to crack, exposing a calculating businessman whose primary allegiance seemed to be to his balance sheet rather than the long-term competitive health of the iconic franchise.

As the mid-2000s progressed, the intricate financial structures McCourt had meticulously erected to separate and leverage the Dodgers' assets began to show pronounced cracks, no longer capable of fully concealing the underlying stress. Reports of delayed payments to vendors and staff, from small local concessionaires to the long-standing stadium grounds crews, and even, in some instances, whispers of slow payments to players or agents, circulated quietly at first among those directly affected, then swelled into public discourse through local media reports. While these concerns were often officially denied or attributed to administrative delays and accounting quirks, they served as concrete indicators that the labyrinthine financial flows, intricately designed to generate capital for McCourt's broader enterprises, were simultaneously and critically restricting the very operational cash flow necessary for the smooth running of a major league baseball team. The strategic decision to carve out the valuable Dodger Stadium parking lots and sell them to Chavez Ravine Properties LLC, and then have the team, through Dodger Holdings LLC, lease them back, was brilliant in its financial engineering for the owner's liquidity. However, it created a continuous and significant outflow of cash from the baseball entity. This steady stream of payments, ostensibly for "rent" or "management fees" flowing from one McCourt-controlled entity to another, meant that substantial revenue generated directly by the team itself – through ticket sales, sponsorships, and concessions – was not necessarily being reinvested in its immediate operational needs, competitive strength, or future development. A significant portion of this diverted revenue was demonstrably directed towards servicing the substantial interest payments on the acquisition debt and other liabilities accrued through his complex corporate empire. This diversion of funds became the philosophical crux of the growing discontent: a fundamental question arose about the team's very purpose. Was the Dodgers primarily a vehicle for its owner's private financial gain and a collateral asset for his real estate ventures, or was it, as generations of fans believed, a cherished community asset meant to be stewarded, invested in, and nurtured for the collective pride and enjoyment of Los Angeles? For many fans, the accumulating evidence increasingly pointed towards the former, breeding a deep-seated cynicism that began to undermine the very foundation of their loyalty. The psychological impact of realizing their financial contributions were seemingly bolstering a personal empire rather than a beloved baseball team was profoundly alienating.

This growing financial strain and the resulting perception of neglect were significantly exacerbated by persistent and increasingly aggressive media scrutiny, which transitioned sharply from initial curiosity about the new owner to incisive investigative reporting. Journalists, particularly from the influential Los Angeles Times—with columnists like Bill Plaschke and investigative reporters like Michael Hiltzik—and later national outlets like ESPN and The Wall Street Journal, began to methodically expose the stark contrast between the team's perceived financial struggles and McCourt's increasingly lavish personal lifestyle. Detailed reports emerged outlining the acquisition and extensive, costly renovation of multiple multi-million-dollar homes in exclusive Los Angeles neighborhoods and Malibu, including the notorious purchase of a $30 million beachfront estate, the conspicuous use of private jets for seemingly routine travel, and a general aura of opulence that seemed jarringly disconnected from the Dodgers' publicly reported financial tightrope walk. This perceived incongruity was galling and infuriating to a fanbase whose ticket purchases, merchandise sales, and unwavering emotional investment ostensibly supported the team. Nevertheless, they saw little tangible return regarding on-field investment or visible commitment to championship pursuit. The psychological effect of this very public display of wealth, juxtaposed starkly with what appeared to be the team's deepening financial constraints and competitive disadvantages, was one of profound anger, resentment, and a corrosive sense of being taken advantage of. The "miserliness" that had been a recurring theme in roster construction, vividly exemplified by the highly criticized departure of Adrián Beltré (as detailed in Chapter 4) despite his career-best performance, was now viewed not merely as a prudent business strategy but as a necessary and direct consequence of the owner's systematic financial extraction from the team's revenue streams. This stark realization fostered a potent and enduring narrative of an owner prioritizing personal enrichment and financial maneuvering over the beloved Dodgers franchise's competitive aspirations and communal pride. The ethical implications of such a divergence between public trust and private gain became a central, unavoidable topic of public debate.

The deepening dissatisfaction among the fan base was anything but passive; it actively manifested in increasingly vocal and organized fan protests, both formal and spontaneous, within the stadium and in the burgeoning digital spaces. Signs highly critical of McCourt and his perceived financial policies began appearing with growing frequency and visibility at Dodger Stadium, often held by disgruntled season ticket holders. Online forums and nascent social media platforms buzzed with impassioned calls for McCourt to sell the team, acting as vital conduits for collective frustration and coordination. While the specific, large-scale public demonstrations that would later characterize the absolute height of the crisis were still years away, the indelible seeds of organized dissent were firmly planted and nurtured during this crucial period. Season ticket holders, who had already endured the bitter taste of betrayal from Drew McCourt's controversial reclassification of seating sections and the perceived insult of the "Twelve-dollar giveaway" (as previously discussed in Chapter 3), were among the most vocal and determined in their opposition. A profound sense of betrayal fueled their escalating anger: They felt their multi-generational loyalty, often spanning decades, was not just unrewarded but was actively and ruthlessly exploited by an ownership that seemed indifferent to their emotional investment. The psychological driver here was the stark violation of an unwritten social contract between the owner and the fanbase; a contract implicitly premised on the idea that fan support, both financial and emotional, would translate directly into a reciprocal commitment to competitive investment, transparency, and respect for the institution. When that sacred contract was perceived to be fundamentally broken by what appeared to be self-serving financial manipulation and a blatant disregard for communal values, loyalty rapidly curdled into deep-seated resentment, and eventually, outright animosity that threatened to fracture the very bond between the team and the city.

Perhaps the most damaging and corrosive aspect of this growing public discontent was the increasing and widely held perception of McCourt's dishonesty and deception. His public statements regarding the team's financial health, often delivered with a carefully constructed facade of optimism, frequently struck critics and careful observers as overly optimistic, if not outright misleading, in light of mounting evidence. He often spoke of the Dodgers being financially sound and perfectly capable of competing at the highest levels, even as relentless media reports detailed mounting debts, repeated restructuring efforts for his various entities, and intricate financial maneuvers that seemed to systematically siphon essential cash away from the team's operational budget. The philosophical argument that emerged was profound: A sports owner, as the custodian of a significant public trust and cultural institution, has an ethical obligation to absolute transparency, primarily when relying heavily on public support, ticket sales, and the very emotional fabric of a community. McCourt's carefully crafted rhetoric, promising future investment, competitive teams, and a renewed focus on fan experience, often clashed sharply and irreconcilably with the stark financial realities consistently revealed by aggressive investigative journalism, creating an insurmountable credibility gap that grew with each passing month. The "specious claims" mentioned in Chapter 5, concerning the flow of funds and the actual state of his various entities, now became a central and deeply damaging component of his fractured public image, unequivocally contributing to a pervasive narrative that he was actively and deliberately misleading the public and, by extension, Major League Baseball itself. Though not yet a direct intervention, Commissioner Bud Selig's office reportedly began to "monitor" the Dodgers' financial situation with increasing scrutiny during this period, signaling growing league concern. The psychological effect of feeling deceived was potent and deeply corrosive, eroding the fundamental trust in professional sports that inextricably binds a fan base to its owner and institution. When fans unequivocally believe they are being lied to or deliberately misled about the financial health and true intentions behind their beloved team, their emotional investment, once a source of civic pride, transforms from unwavering support to a powerful and indignant sense of betrayal, anger, and utter disillusionment. This perception of deceit, rooted in a systematic lack of transparency, was a constant and poisonous undercurrent that profoundly contaminated the relationship between McCourt and the entire Dodgers community, turning every financial decision, every public statement, and every on-field struggle into a potential source of inflamed public controversy and further erosion of confidence.

The confluence of growing financial strain, obvious fan protests, relentless media scrutiny of his finances, and the increasingly corrosive perception of his fundamental dishonesty and deception fundamentally transformed the nature of Frank McCourt's ownership. The initial, albeit fragile, optimism had entirely dissipated, replaced by a festering resentment that relentlessly eroded the Dodgers' institutional goodwill. This process proved more damaging than any on-field loss. This period marked a critical juncture in which the philosophical debate about the purpose and ethical obligations of sports ownership became acutely relevant and publicly debated in Los Angeles. Was the Dodgers merely a readily accessible vehicle for McCourt's complex real estate and personal financial empire, designed for leveraging and extraction, or did it remain a public institution demanding a different, higher standard of stewardship and community engagement? The psychological impact of this prolonged discontent was severe and enduring, resulting in a deep and seemingly irreparable fracture in the relationship between the owner and the fan base. This schism would prove incredibly difficult, if not impossible, to bridge through any conventional means. The sophisticated financial structures, initially a source of McCourt's ability to acquire the team, became increasingly seen by the public and eventually by the league itself as instruments of extraction, opacity, and financial manipulation. The "miserliness" was no longer just a critique of player salaries, but had evolved into a damning indictment of a broader financial strategy that seemed to unequivocally prioritize personal gain and debt servicing over competitive integrity and community trust. This growing discontent, deeply fueled by a pervasive sense of deception and disillusionment, not only defined the latter half of McCourt's tenure but also ominously foreshadowed the profound crisis that would eventually engulf the entire franchise, dramatically demonstrating the peril of an owner's financial philosophy clashing so fundamentally and irreconcilably with the deeply held values and expectations of a devoted public.

Chapter 7
The Divorce

The simmering discontent that had long percolated beneath the surface of Frank McCourt's ownership of the Los Angeles Dodgers erupted into a full-blown public conflagration with the dramatic and profoundly acrimonious divorce proceedings between him and his then-wife, Jamie McCourt. What began as a private marital dispute swiftly morphed into a devastating public spectacle, a legal and financial battle of unprecedented scale that directly and irrevocably impacted the team's ownership, precarious financial stability, and the very perception of the iconic franchise. This chapter details how a personal rupture became the ultimate catalyst that laid bare the fragile foundation of McCourt's empire, exposing the intricate web of debt, leveraging, and alleged deception that had, until then, largely remained hidden behind corporate veils.

The divorce proceedings, initiated by Jamie McCourt in October 2009, sent shockwaves not only through the McCourt family but throughout Major League Baseball and the entire

Los Angeles community. Jamie, who had been appointed CEO of the Dodgers by Frank shortly after their acquisition of the team, claimed to be a co-owner, entitled to half of the Dodgers and their associated assets under California's community property laws. Frank, however, vehemently disputed this, asserting that a post-nuptial agreement signed in 2004, shortly after they acquired the team, stipulated that the Dodgers were his separate property. His subsequent abrupt firing of Jamie as CEO in the same month further escalated public animosity, transforming what might have been a private settlement into an intensely public and protracted legal war. The initial shock quickly gave way to a voracious public appetite for the unfolding drama, as the highest echelons of professional sports were forced to witness a beloved franchise being dissected in a courthouse. The philosophical question was whether a team, perceived by many as a public trust, could be so inextricably tied to its owner's personal financial and legal battles that it risked its very stability.

The legal battle over the Dodgers' ownership hinged critically on the validity of that post-nuptial agreement. Jamie McCourt's legal team argued vehemently that the agreement, which ostensibly gave Frank sole ownership of the Dodgers in exchange for other properties, was flawed, misleading, and therefore invalid. Central to their argument was the revelation that Frank had allegedly presented five different versions of the agreement, some containing subtle yet significant changes that blurred the lines of asset ownership. This egregious revelation of multiple, conflicting documents unequivocally shattered Frank's claims of a clear, separate ownership. The protracted courtroom drama, presided over by various judges over the years, served as an unprecedented public audit of McCourt's entire financial architecture, exposing the core of his "real estate play" (as detailed in Chapter 5). The concept of community property became the legal battleground, with Jamie asserting her marital right to half of the assets acquired during their marriage, including the Dodgers. Frank's tenacious defense, resting on the validity of the shifting post-nuptial document, ultimately failed when a court ruled that the various versions of the agreement created ambiguity, rendering it unenforceable. This legal setback was not just a personal blow to Frank but a devastating public dismantling of his carefully constructed financial narrative. It cast a harsh light on his earlier "specious claims" of sole ownership and financial rectitude. The psychological impact on Frank was undoubtedly immense, as his control over his most prized asset slipped, and his carefully cultivated image as a shrewd, singular operator was publicly shredded.

Beyond the ownership dispute, the divorce proceedings forced an unprecedented and utterly humiliating public unveiling of the Dodgers' financial stability or its perilous lack thereof. The legal discovery process required complete transparency into McCourt's complex financial affairs, compelling him to disclose intimate details about his debts, loans, and personal expenditures that had previously been shielded by corporate complexity. In these court documents, the true extent of the Dodgers' financial leveraging and Frank McCourt's reliance on the team's revenues became horrifyingly clear. Revelations included the staggering amounts of debt tied to the team and its assets, the extent to which McCourt had taken personal loans secured by the Dodgers' future revenue streams (like television rights), and the astonishing sums that had been siphoned from the team through "management fees" and other related-party transactions to service his lifestyle. For instance, court records revealed personal spending that included upwards of $10 million on multiple luxurious homes and over $2 million on private jet travel. The accusation, repeatedly levied by Jamie's legal team and amplified by the media, that Frank had treated the Dodgers like his "personal ATM," was corroborated by the financial records he was forced to disclose. This public exposure of his dire financial straits and the extent of his spending, often reaching tens of millions of dollars for lavish homes, private jet travel, and other luxuries, further inflamed the public's perception of his "miserliness" (as discussed in Chapter 6) regarding team investment. The philosophical implications were stark: The divorce court became the ultimate arbiter of public trust, revealing how an owner's private financial decisions could utterly jeopardize a civic institution.

The direct impact of these highly public and financially draining divorce proceedings on the team's ownership and operational stability was catastrophic. The legal uncertainty hanging over the franchise created an environment of paralyzing instability. With the team's ultimate ownership in question and a significant portion of its assets potentially subject to division, the Dodgers could not make major financial decisions crucial for a competitive baseball team. Player signings, long-term contracts, significant stadium investments (beyond cosmetic changes), and even routine operational expenditures were all put on hold or drastically curtailed. This paralysis directly affected the team's ability to compete on the field, further validating the long-held concerns about McCourt's "miserliness" and undermining the efforts of managers like Joe Torre and Don Mattingly (from Chapter 4) to build a winning culture amidst the chaos. The psychological toll on the team—players, coaches, and staff—was immense. They operated under constant uncertainty, their professional careers tied to an organization whose very existence seemed imperiled by a marital dispute. Morale undoubtedly suffered, and the focus on winning baseball games was inevitably overshadowed by the daily headlines detailing the owner's legal battles and financial woes.

The fan base, already disillusioned by years of perceived neglect and questionable financial practices, witnessed the franchise they cherished being torn apart by a private feud playing out on a very public stage. It deepened their sense of betrayal and disgust, transforming growing discontent into outright outrage. The philosophical idea of a public trust consumed by private turmoil reached its painful zenith. The revelations of McCourt's alleged dishonesty and deception, particularly regarding the varying versions of the post-nuptial agreement, further cemented the perception that he was fundamentally untrustworthy and that the team's financial health had been deliberately obscured. The league itself, spearheaded by Commissioner Bud Selig, grew increasingly concerned about the Dodgers' viability and the potential damage to the integrity of Major League Baseball. Selig's office began issuing public statements expressing "serious concerns" about the team's financial stability and the ongoing ownership dispute, signaling a clear shift towards potential intervention. The public spectacle of the divorce, the undeniable financial revelations, and the legal quagmire that threatened the team's operations left MLB with little choice but to intervene. The psychological pressure on McCourt mounted as he faced not only his estranged wife's legal assault but also the formidable might of the league's commissioner. The divorce, therefore, was not merely a personal tragedy; it was the ultimate public unraveling of Frank McCourt's ownership, exposing the fragility of his financial model and demonstrating how individual avarice and marital discord could bring a revered sports institution to the brink of collapse, necessitating an unprecedented intervention to preserve its very existence.

Chapter 8
MLB Intervention

The protracted and increasingly acrimonious divorce proceedings of Frank and Jamie McCourt had, by early 2011, stripped away any remaining pretense of stability surrounding the Dodgers' ownership. The financial revelations unearthed in divorce court, laid bare for the world to see, painted a devastating picture of immense debt, systemic leveraging of team assets, and a troubling commingling of personal and team finances. It was this undeniable public spectacle of financial peril, coupled with the team's ongoing inability to meet its operational obligations, that finally compelled Major League Baseball Commissioner Bud Selig to execute an unprecedented and decisive intervention. This pivotal moment marked a dramatic shift in the balance of power between an owner and the league, asserting the philosophical principle that a sports franchise, even a privately owned one, ultimately serves a collective interest that transcends individual proprietary rights.

The precursors to Commissioner Selig's drastic action had been building for years, culminating in the public and damaging financial disclosures from the divorce. As meticulously detailed in Chapter 6, the signs of economic strain had grown from whispers to undeniable facts: reports of delayed vendor payments, the perceived "miserliness" in team investment despite burgeoning revenues, and the glaring incongruity between the team's reported fiscal tightrope walk and McCourt's lavish personal spending. Chapter 7 further illuminated the extent of the leveraging and the internal financial manipulations that treated the Dodgers as a personal ATM. For a considerable period, MLB attempted to work with McCourt behind the scenes, urging him to resolve his financial quagmire and bring stability back to the franchise. However, his escalating legal battles with Jamie, inability to secure conventional financing without further encumbering the team, and the looming prospect of defaulting on vital obligations (such as player payroll) left the league with few options. The psychological pressure on Selig and MLB's hierarchy was immense; the Dodgers were an iconic franchise, synonymous with professional baseball's historical tapestry, and allowing it to spiral into financial ruin would inflict irreparable damage not only on the team's brand but on the fundamental integrity and public perception of Major League Baseball itself.

ALLEN SCHERY

On April 20, 2011, Commissioner Selig formally announced his decision to take control of the Dodgers' day-to-day operations. His reasons were clear and resolute: "deep concerns regarding the finances and the operations of the Los Angeles Dodgers." He underscored the need to "protect the franchise's best interests, its fans, and all of Major League Baseball." This move was not without historical precedent in other sports. However, for baseball, it was a dramatic assertion of power, indicating that the league, as a collective enterprise, could supersede the absolute rights of an individual owner when the very fabric of the game was perceived to be at risk. To execute this takeover, Selig appointed Tom Schieffer, a respected former Texas Rangers president and ambassador, as the independent monitor to oversee all of the Dodgers' business and financial affairs. Schieffer's mandate was broad: to ensure the team met its obligations, to stabilize its operations, and to conduct a thorough financial investigation. The philosophical justification for such an intervention rested on the notion that while baseball teams are privately owned, they are also part of a larger, interdependent league structure, a shared enterprise whose collective reputation and financial health depend on the stability of each member club. Allowing one franchise to collapse due to mismanagement was deemed an unacceptable risk to the sport. This decision sent a clear psychological message to all other owners: their property rights, while significant, were not absolute when faced with potential harm to the common good of Major League Baseball.

Frank McCourt, however, was not one to yield control quietly. His response to Selig's intervention was swift, aggressive, and characterized by a staunch belief in his private property rights. He immediately launched a series of legal battles against Major League Baseball, accusing Selig of overreach, violating his contractual rights as an owner, and unjustifiably seizing his private business. McCourt's legal arguments centered on the idea that the Dodgers were his assets, legally acquired, and that the league had no right to interfere with their management, notably when he maintained that he could meet his financial obligations. He famously argued that the league's intervention stemmed from personal animosity or a desire to force a sale at an undervalued price. These court filings and counter-filings created a secondary, parallel battleground played out in federal courtrooms, often running concurrently with his divorce proceedings. MLB's counterarguments, rooted in the "best interests of baseball" clause embedded in the league's constitution, asserted that McCourt's actions and the team's financial instability were actively damaging the brand of the Dodgers and, by extension, the entire league. They argued that McCourt's financial maneuvers, including using future media rights as collateral for personal loans, demonstrated a disregard for the franchise's long-term health and the league's collective well-being. The psychological toll of this dual legal warfare—battling his estranged wife and the powerful league simultaneously—must have been immense for McCourt, a man accustomed to being in control. For the league, it was a necessary, though costly, assertion of its authority, demonstrating a resolute stance against ownership perceived as detrimental to the sport.

As the legal battles raged, McCourt desperately attempted to retain control and refinance his debt. His most prominent effort involved a proposed 17-year, $3 billion television rights deal with Fox Sports. This deal, he argued, would provide the necessary capital to meet his financial obligations, resolve his debts, and inject funds back into the team, thereby negating the need for MLB's oversight. However, after a thorough review, MLB unequivocally blocked the deal, citing that a substantial portion of the upfront payment was intended for McCourt's personal use, including paying off his divorce settlement with Jamie. This rejection highlighted the league's firm stance: any new financing had to benefit the team demonstrably and not merely prop up McCourt's financial house of cards. MLB viewed the Fox deal as another example of McCourt leveraging the Dodgers' future for his immediate needs, perpetuating the very problem they were trying to solve. The escalating financial desperation, made public through the ongoing legal skirmishes, painted a clear picture of an owner unable to secure traditional financing and whose every proposed solution seemed to involve mortgaging the team's long-term future. This impasse, along with the ongoing inability to meet operational payments, pushed Selig toward the ultimate resolution: a forced sale.

MLB initiated the forced sale process, though technically, it became a mediated sale process to avoid further prolonged litigation with McCourt. This decision triggered an extraordinary search for a new owner, setting the stage for one of sports history's most high-profile bidding wars. The sale process was meticulously managed, drawing interest from prominent figures and investment groups across the nation. The philosophical implications of selling an iconic team under such duress were significant: It underscored that owning a major league franchise was not just a private right, but a privilege accompanied by immense responsibilities to the league, the game, and the community. Despite its recent turmoil, the bidding process was a testament to the enduring value and allure of the Dodgers franchise. Ultimately, the team was sold in a record-breaking deal that shattered previous valuations for sports franchises. The winning bid, totaling an astonishing $2.15 billion, was placed by Guggenheim Baseball Management. This group included influential figures such as Mark Walter, Stan Kasten (a highly respected baseball executive), and the beloved Lakers legend Earvin "Magic" Johnson.

The record-breaking sale price, far exceeding initial estimates, was a profound psychological affirmation of the Dodgers' underlying value and brand strength, demonstrating that the fundamental asset remained incredibly desirable despite the financial turmoil. The sale signaled a new beginning for the fan base, bringing a profound sense of relief after years of anxiety, disillusionment, and public embarrassment. The psychological burden lifted from the players, staff, and loyal supporters was immense, replaced by renewed hope and optimism for the future. For Frank McCourt, the sale represented the bitter end of his ownership, a public acknowledgment of defeat in his battle against MLB, and the inevitable consequence of his unsustainable financial model. His psychological state during this period, when he lost ultimate control over his most prized asset, must have been one of profound frustration, even as he walked away with a significant personal profit from the sale, primarily due to the team's inflated valuation and the repayment of his various debts. The philosophical lesson from this dramatic intervention and sale was clear: while professional sports teams are privately owned, the league, through its commissioner, holds ultimate authority to protect the collective interests of the sport. It firmly established that ownership is a privilege that comes with a powerful implicit social contract, and a direct threat to that contract, through financial mismanagement or egregious public conduct, would ultimately be met with firm, decisive action. The Dodgers' saga under McCourt became a defining case study in the evolving relationship between private ownership and the public trust inherent in professional sports.

Chapter 9
The Sale

The tumultuous saga of Frank McCourt's ownership, brought to a dramatic head by the highly public divorce proceedings and Major League Baseball's unprecedented intervention, culminated in the monumental sale of the Los Angeles Dodgers. This final act was not merely a transaction; it was a watershed moment that closed a painful, embarrassing chapter in the franchise's illustrious history and simultaneously ushered in an era of renewed hope and, perhaps, a more enlightened approach to sports stewardship. The extraordinary circumstances surrounding the sale, driven by the league's imperative to restore institutional stability and the overwhelming need to resolve McCourt's intractable financial and legal quagmire definitively, transformed what would typically be a relatively private business negotiation into a highly publicized, high-stakes global auction, scrutinized by millions.

The genesis of this extraordinary sale lay directly in the profound and systemic financial instability that had engulfed the

Dodgers, a crisis relentlessly exposed with undeniable clarity during Frank and Jamie McCourt's divorce proceedings (as detailed in Chapter 7). Commissioner Bud Selig's decisive and historic action to take control of the team's day-to-day operations in April 2011, an unprecedented move marking the first time a central league commissioner had seized control of a team from an owner, was the ultimate, unequivocal acknowledgment that McCourt, despite his fervent and protracted desire to retain ownership, could not stabilize the franchise's hemorrhaging finances or definitively resolve his crippling personal legal disputes without gravely imperiling the team's very existence and, by extension, the broader integrity and public trust of Major League Baseball. The league's mandate for sale was clear and non-negotiable: the Dodgers required a financially sound owner, untainted by the previous controversies, who possessed the capital, vision, and commitment to restore the team's standing, invest robustly in its future, and mend the deeply fractured relationship with its fanbase. Ultimately, this mandate led to the team's Chapter 11 bankruptcy filing, which formally paved the way for a court-supervised auction. Thus began the bidding process, which rapidly evolved into a global phenomenon, transforming a typical business acquisition into a spectacle that captivated the financial markets and the entire sports world, drawing immense media attention and public fascination. It stood as a powerful testament to the enduring intrinsic value and iconic status of the Dodgers brand, demonstrating its remarkable resilience even after years of unprecedented turmoil.

The bidding process was nothing short of a spectacle, a rigorous, multi-staged auction meticulously orchestrated by Major League Baseball and its appointed financial advisors from the Blackstone Group, designed to extract the maximum possible value for the distressed franchise while ensuring a stable and reputable future. The number and astonishing diversity of interested parties ranged from seasoned sports owners and private equity titans with vast portfolios to high-profile celebrity figures, revered sports legends, and influential local entrepreneurs. This intense competitive frenzy vividly highlighted the unique, almost mystical, allure of owning a storied franchise like the Dodgers. This entity represents a quantifiable business asset, a profound cultural touchstone, and a civic institution. Each prospective ownership group, comprising billionaires with seemingly limitless resources, astute sports executives with proven track records of building successful organizations, and figures with deep, authentic ties to the vibrant Los Angeles community, diligently navigated multiple rounds of stringent vetting and due diligence. This thorough process ensured that not only absolute financial capacity but also a long-term vision for the team's future, a clean reputation, and a genuine commitment to community engagement were paramount considerations. The systematically escalating offers in each successive round of bidding reflected not just the formidable economic potential of the Dodgers—particularly its vast, untapped media rights and the immense developmental value of the Chavez Ravine real estate—but also the powerful psychological desire to acquire such a revered global brand. For the myriad bidders, it was profoundly more than just a calculated investment; it was an unparalleled opportunity to claim a significant piece of American history, to wield immense influence within the exclusive, tightly knit club of Major League Baseball ownership, and to become the highly visible custodian of a treasured civic institution. This auction's sheer intensity and record-breaking nature vividly underscore the philosophical truth that while a professional sports franchise is undoubtedly a business entity, it carries immense, intangible value rooted in community identity, collective memory, and historical significance that consistently transcends purely financial metrics. The competitive drive and ego inherent in such a high-stakes competition further inflated the final price, pushing it far beyond conventional valuations.

Among the numerous formidable contenders, including highly respected figures like Steven Cohen of SAC Capital, Peter Guber (co-owner of the Golden State Warriors and LAFC), and business mogul Rick Caruso, the eventual winning bid came from Guggenheim Baseball Management. This strategically assembled consortium brilliantly combined diverse strengths to present an utterly irresistible offer. The group was led by Mark Walter, a highly successful and financially discreet CEO of Guggenheim Partners, whose immense personal capital and institutional backing provided the necessary financial muscle and long-term stability that Major League Baseball so desperately sought. Walter's investment philosophy, characterized by patience and strategic growth, promised a stark departure from the short-term leveraging tactics of the previous ownership. Crucially, the group also included Stan Kasten, a highly respected and experienced baseball executive known for his successful tenures in transforming struggling franchises, such as the Atlanta Braves and Washington Nationals, into contenders. Kasten's inclusion immediately signaled a serious, professional commitment to sound baseball operations and a return to experienced, data-driven management, directly addressing the systemic concerns about the perceived inefficiencies and amateurish nature of the previous regime's business side. However, perhaps the most strategically brilliant and psychologically impactful inclusion was that of Earvin "Magic" Johnson. A universally beloved Los Angeles icon and a former Lakers superstar, Magic Johnson's presence instantly provided a powerful, emotional, and authentic bridge to the deeply alienated fan base. After years of McCourt's perceived aloofness, financial machinations, and the painful public spectacle, the symbolic return of a local legend—a figure synonymous with Los Angeles sporting greatness and community engagement—offered unparalleled credibility, goodwill, and genuine civic connection. His involvement promised a fundamental and much-needed shift in the owner-fan relationship, from one of distrust and perceived exploitation to one of shared passion, renewed pride, and collective aspiration. The thoughtful composition of this group—combining formidable financial power, proven baseball acumen, and unparalleled local celebrity—was a strategic masterstroke that resonated deeply and authentically with both the league and the profoundly disillusioned public. It was a conscious effort to rebuild trust and re-establish the social contract between the team and its city.

The sale officially concluded on March 27, 2012, with a staggering and unprecedented price tag of $2.15 billion. This colossal figure immediately shattered all previous records for the sale of a professional sports franchise, an astonishing valuation that, on its surface, seemed to defy the team's recent turbulent history and dire financial woes. The sheer magnitude of the price was a testament to several interconnected factors: the enduring, almost mythical, power of the Dodgers' brand, its prime location within the vast and affluent Los Angeles media market, the immense and largely untapped potential for a lucrative new regional television rights deal (which Guggenheim would swiftly secure and leverage), and the undeniable underlying value of the Chavez Ravine real estate that McCourt had so astutely recognized and fragmented. The fiercely competitive bidding process, with multiple well-funded groups relentlessly pushing each other to offer unprecedented sums, contributed significantly to the final price. The philosophical implications of such a record-breaking valuation for a professional sports team were profound: it unequivocally confirmed their elevated status as premier global entertainment assets, far surpassing mere baseball clubs. It solidified the notion that professional sports franchises are not just businesses but immensely valuable, limited-supply commodities. They increasingly attract investment from the world's wealthiest individuals and most sophisticated financial institutions, viewing them as status symbols and highly profitable ventures. For Frank McCourt, despite the palpable public humiliation of the forced sale and the public scrutiny of his business practices, the transaction ultimately offered a surprisingly lucrative exit. The prodigious sale proceeds were meticulously allocated: first, to satisfy the substantial divorce settlement with Jamie McCourt; then, to repay his legion of creditors and lenders who had financed his initial leveraged acquisition and subsequent financial maneuvers; and finally, leaving him with a significant personal profit, reportedly in the hundreds of millions of dollars. This financial outcome, where an owner whose management was explicitly deemed detrimental by the league still walked away with considerable fortune, ignited widespread public outrage and a further public debate on the complex nature of sports ownership, accountability, and the inherent risks versus rewards in such high-stakes ventures.

The announcement of the sale and the subsequent formal transfer of ownership to Guggenheim Baseball Management ignited an immense, palpable sense of collective relief and widespread celebration among the Dodgers faithful. For years, the fanbase had stoically endured a relentless barrage of negative headlines, public financial scandals, and the profound emotional toll of witnessing their beloved franchise embroiled in bitter personal and legal disputes that overshadowed the game. The crushing psychological burden that had weighed heavily on them was finally and comprehensively lifted, replaced by a profound sense of a new beginning, a genuine and deeply felt belief that the team was once again in "good hands"—hands that symbolized stability, investment, and a renewed commitment to winning. The prominent presence of Magic Johnson primarily acted as a powerful symbolic balm, promising a return to the community-oriented spirit and fan engagement that many felt had been tragically lost under the previous regime. This pivotal moment marked the start of a critical new era for the Dodgers, symbolizing a change in ownership and a fundamental shift in the philosophical approach to stewardship. The pervasive perception was that the team would now be managed by individuals prioritizing on-field success, transparent community engagement, and long-term institutional stability over transient personal financial maneuvering. For Major League Baseball, the successful and relatively swift resolution of the Dodgers crisis was a significant, hard-won victory, demonstrating the league's robust ability to intervene decisively and effectively to protect its collective interests and the fundamental integrity of the game. It served as a powerful and enduring precedent, unequivocally reaffirming the commissioner's ultimate authority over individual owners when their actions or financial instability threatened the well-being and reputation of the entire sport. The sale of the Dodgers, therefore, became a powerful, defining case study in the complex, often contentious, but ultimately vital relationship between private ownership and the profound public trust inherent in professional sports, highlighting the enduring power of an iconic brand to transcend even its deepest periods of adversity.

Chapter 10
A New Era

The dawn of a new era for the Los Angeles Dodgers arrived with the official transfer of ownership to Guggenheim Baseball Management in March 2012, a moment greeted with a collective sigh of relief and an almost palpable sense of euphoria across the sprawling Los Angeles landscape. After years of financial turmoil, public embarrassment, and a deeply fractured relationship between the franchise and its fervent fanbase, the arrival of the new ownership group, spearheaded by the financial might of Mark Walter and the iconic presence of Magic Johnson, symbolized a profound philosophical shift. It was no longer an ownership primarily focused on leveraging real estate assets or navigating intricate personal legal battles; at least in its stated intent and immediate actions, it was ownership committed to restoring the Dodgers' competitive glory and robustly reconnecting with the community. The psychological impact of this transition was immediate and transformative, systematically replacing widespread cynicism and disengagement with a burgeoning sense of hope, renewed civic pride, and an eager anticipation for a brighter future.

The immediate changes enacted under the new ownership were swift, decisive, and meticulously designed to directly address the most pressing issues that had systematically plagued the franchise under Frank McCourt's stewardship. Foremost among these reforms was a dramatic and unequivocal commitment to financial stability and sustained investment. Gone were the days of delayed payments to loyal vendors, the unsettling whispers of impending payroll issues, or the constant need for McCourt to refinance his precarious debt; the Guggenheim group, fortified by its vast institutional financial resources, immediately injected substantial capital into the team. This influx of funds systematically cleared all outstanding debts, including the complex divorce settlement with Jamie McCourt, and ensured robust, consistent operational funding. This financial liberation allowed the Dodgers to finally shed the stifling shackles of McCourt's well-documented "miserliness" (as discussed in earlier chapters) and aggressively pursue top-tier talent in both the free-agent market and through strategic trades. The philosophical shift was undeniable and invigorating: money would no longer impede achieving competitive excellence. It was not merely about spending but about spending strategically, judiciously, and with a clear, long-term vision for sustainable success, representing a stark and welcome contrast to the previous regime's fragmented, short-term financial maneuvering. The psychological effect of this newfound financial solidity was profound, reverberating internally within the entire Dodgers organization and externally among the long-suffering fanbase. Players and coaching staff could now fully focus on the intricacies of baseball, liberated from the constant, gnawing anxiety of financial instability. At the same time, fans saw tangible, unambiguous evidence that their beloved team was once again being treated as a premier, global franchise worthy of significant and sustained investment. It reestablished a fundamental trust that had eroded over years of perceived financial neglect.

Beyond financial stabilization, the new ownership immediately prioritized rebuilding the team's severely tarnished reputation and reconnecting with the disillusioned fan base. The strategic inclusion and evident presence of Earvin "Magic" Johnson proved instrumental in this critical endeavor. As a universally beloved figure synonymous with Los Angeles sporting success, profound community engagement, and an unwavering commitment to excellence, Johnson voluntarily became the vibrant, accessible public face of the new ownership. He tirelessly engaged with fans at every opportunity, appeared at countless community events across the vast city, and articulated a compelling vision of shared purpose and collective ambition. His infectious charisma, genuine passion for Los Angeles sports, and unparalleled ability to connect with people served as a powerful and much-needed antidote to the years of perceived aloofness, legalistic stonewalling, and self-interested financial maneuvering under McCourt. It was a deliberate and deeply insightful psychological strategy to systematically re-establish the broken social contract between the team and its community. The philosophical message communicated was clear and resonant: The Dodgers were, once again, a cherished public trust, an integral and invaluable part of the city's identity, and the new owners demonstrably understood and wholeheartedly embraced this profound civic responsibility. This renewed commitment extended beyond mere appearances to more tangible and visible efforts, such as significant, highly publicized stadium improvements beyond superficial cosmetic changes. These enhancements focused strategically on fundamentally improving fan experience with modern amenities, upgraded infrastructure, and careful preservation of the ballpark's iconic, historic charm. The entire atmosphere at Dodger Stadium underwent a palpable transformation, shifting from one of simmering resentment and quiet resignation to one of vibrant, renewed enthusiasm, collective optimism, and boisterous celebration, as attendance figures began a consistent climb, powerfully reflecting the rekindled connection between the team and its city.

However, the most visible, immediate, and impactful change was the dramatic resurgence of the Dodgers on the field, driven by an aggressive yet strategically astute approach to player acquisition. Liberated entirely from the crippling financial constraints that had defined the McCourt era, the Guggenheim group immediately signaled its unequivocal intent to compete at the absolute highest level of Major League Baseball. This bold commitment was exemplified by high-profile trades and lucrative free-agent signings that sent veritable shockwaves through the entire league, fundamentally altering the competitive landscape. In August 2012, just a mere few months after officially taking over the franchise, the Dodgers executed a monumental, franchise-altering trade with the Boston Red Sox, acquiring bona fide stars such as first baseman Adrian Gonzalez, veteran outfielder Carl Crawford, seasoned pitcher Josh Beckett, and versatile infielder Nick Punto. This blockbuster deal, a direct and resounding reversal of the previous regime's chronic parsimony (which had notoriously seen a homegrown star like Adrián Beltré depart), not only brought significant, immediate talent to Los Angeles but also willingly absorbed their substantial long-term contracts, demonstrating the new ownership's unprecedented willingness to spend strategically for competitive advantage. It was swiftly followed by other significant acquisitions, including the highly anticipated signing of Korean pitching sensation Hyun-Jin Ryu and, in subsequent years, other high-profile, impactful players who solidified the roster. The philosophical approach underlying these moves was clear and uncompromising: assemble the best possible roster, regardless of the financial cost, with the singular, overriding goal of competing fiercely for a World Series championship every year. The psychological impact on the team, from the clubhouse to the dugout, was immediate and immensely positive; players felt a profound, renewed sense of purpose, professional validation, and an unwavering belief that the organization was now truly committed to winning at all costs. For the long-suffering fan base, these bold, decisive moves were a powerful and deeply felt validation of their renewed hope, transforming abstract promises into tangible, high-caliber on-field talent that sparked immediate excitement.

The impact of this aggressive and sustained investment in talent was almost instantaneous, translating directly into on-field success. The Dodgers, under the continued and steady management of Don Mattingly (who had admirably navigated the tumultuous and uncertain final year of McCourt's ownership with remarkable resilience), made a dramatic and thrilling surge in the latter half of the 2012 season, falling just agonizingly short of a playoff berth but unequivocally signaling their formidable intent for the coming years. The true, sustained resurgence began in 2013, when the team, powered by a dominant pitching staff featuring the rapidly ascending Clayton Kershaw (who continued his inexorable ascent to superstardom and Cy Young glory) and the newly acquired talent, captured the coveted National League West division title with authority. This pivotal triumph marked the auspicious beginning of an unprecedented and historic run of sustained success, with the Dodgers consistently contending for and winning division titles in subsequent years, firmly establishing themselves as one of Major League Baseball's perennial powerhouses. The philosophical shift was vividly evident in their sustained performance: The team was no longer merely trying to be competitive or hoping for a lucky streak; it was strategically built, financially empowered, and organizationally aligned to dominate its division and contend fiercely for the World Series every single season. The psychological effect of this prolonged and consistent success was immense, serving as a powerful balm that healed old wounds of disappointment and rekindled the deep, generational passion of the Dodgers' faithful. Attendance at Dodger Stadium soared to league-leading levels, merchandise sales skyrocketed, and the iconic ballpark once again became an electric, vibrant atmosphere, a true and undeniable home-field advantage. The years of perceived "miserliness," financial instability, and emotional detachment were systematically replaced by a pervasive sense of abundance, unwavering commitment, and a renewed belief in the team's boundless potential.

Beyond the immediate and impactful player acquisitions, the new ownership also demonstrated a sagacious long-term vision by investing heavily and strategically in the team's infrastructure and long-term sustainability. It included significant and visible upgrades to Dodger Stadium, meticulously focusing on modernizing its facilities, vastly improving fan amenities, and preserving the ballpark's cherished, iconic charm and rich history. They also poured substantial resources and strategic planning into revitalizing the team's player development system and expanding its international scouting networks, recognizing with prescience that sustained, perennial success at the significant league level required a robust, self-sufficient pipeline of homegrown talent, not just a reliance on expensive free-agent signings. A cornerstone of this long-term strategy was the landmark 25-year, $8.35 billion regional television rights deal with Time

Warner Cable, secured shortly after the acquisition, providing unprecedented financial stability for decades to come. This holistic and forward-thinking approach reflected a philosophical understanding that a truly successful and enduring franchise requires comprehensive investment at every level of the organization, from the major league roster and coaching staff down to the grassroots of amateur scouting and player development. The psychological message conveyed by this far-reaching investment was one of foresight, stability, and unwavering long-term commitment, assuring fans that the Dodgers were not simply chasing ephemeral immediate wins but were thoughtfully and deliberately building a sustainable dynasty designed to endure for decades. The stark contrast with the previous era, where such vital long-term investments were often sacrificed for fleeting, short-term financial gains or personal advantage, was undeniably evident and profoundly reassuring to a fan base yearning for stability.

The "new era" under Guggenheim Baseball Management represented a profound and multifaceted philosophical and psychological transformation for the Los Angeles Dodgers organization. It was a deliberate, comprehensive, and ultimately successful attempt to systematically reverse the deep and pervasive damage inflicted by years of financial mismanagement, public discord, and perceived neglect. The immediate, decisive changes—characterized by robust financial stability, aggressive and intelligent player investment, a genuine and unwavering renewed focus on comprehensive community engagement, and an unwavering commitment to long-term infrastructure and player development—collectively fostered a powerful and undeniable resurgence of the field. It also brought about a deep and lasting healing of the once-fractured relationship with the loyal fanbase. The team's consistent competitive success, marked by division titles and deep playoff runs, became the ultimate and most compelling validation of this new, enlightened approach, irrefutably proving that a clear vision, robust financial backing, a deep understanding of organizational excellence, and, critically, a genuine appreciation for the unique and sacred bond between a team and its city were the authentic, indispensable ingredients for restoring a storied franchise to its rightful place at the absolute pinnacle of professional sports. The dark, lingering shadow of Frank McCourt's tumultuous and controversial ownership had finally, unequivocally lifted, replaced by the bright, promising dawn of a revitalized and seemingly indomitable Dodgers dynasty poised for sustained greatness.

Chapter 11

Aftermath

The tumultuous chapter of Frank McCourt's ownership of the Los Angeles Dodgers closed with the record-breaking sale of the franchise in 2012, yet for McCourt himself, it was far from the final act. Instead, it marked a strategic pivot, re-channeling his formidable entrepreneurial drive and financial acumen into new ventures within and outside professional sports. His post-Dodgers trajectory offers a fascinating study in resilience, adaptation, and the enduring power of leveraging assets, even those seemingly divested, against public scrutiny and personal transformation. The philosophical question that lingered after his contentious departure from baseball was whether his bruising experiences in Los Angeles had tempered his audacious approach or if his fundamental strategies of shrewd financial engineering and asset manipulation would be applied with renewed vigor to new arenas, unburdened by the specific pressures of American Major League Baseball.

Frank McCourt's most prominent and high-profile post-Dodgers venture has been his acquisition of Olympique Marseille, a storied French professional football (soccer) club he finalized in 2016. This bold move into European sports signaled his continued, indeed unflagging, interest in high-profile sports ownership, albeit now operating within a different league, a distinct financial ecosystem, and a new, fiercely passionate cultural context. The acquisition of Marseille, a club steeped in history with a fervent, almost visceral, fanbase that fills the venerable Stade Vélodrome with thunderous chants and vivid flares, mirrored critical aspects of his initial Dodgers purchase: a venerated yet somewhat underperforming asset with clear, perceived untapped potential and a passionate, demanding public eager for renewed glory. His public statements upon acquiring Marseille echoed, often uncannily, his initial rhetoric upon arriving in Los Angeles a decade prior: emphasizing an unwavering commitment to competitive success, promising substantial investment in the club's infrastructure and roster, and articulating a profound desire to connect authentically with the deeply devoted fanbase. Psychologically, this venture offered McCourt a powerful opportunity for a genuinely fresh start, a chance to apply his ownership philosophies and business strategies far from the immediate, intense scrutiny and lingering baggage that had so relentlessly defined his final, embattled years with the Dodgers. It allowed him to meticulously re-establish a narrative of successful sports stewardship, operating comfortably beyond the critical gaze of American baseball media and the specific pressures of the MLB commissioner's office. This significant diversification into European football also represented a strategic expansion of his burgeoning global portfolio, positioning him as a substantial, albeit still controversial, player in the ever-growing international sports business landscape, a testament to his enduring ambition to operate at the absolute highest levels of professional sports, where significant capital investments meet massive public interest. He launched what he termed the "Champions Project" for Marseille, outlining ambitious plans for substantial investment in new players, academy development, and a renewed pursuit of domestic and European titles, attempting to replicate the kind of transformative impact he had initially envisioned, though never fully realized, for the Dodgers. However, similar to his Dodgers tenure, his time with Marseille has been marked by periods of fervent fan protest regarding financial transparency and perceived underinvestment, demonstrating that the challenges of balancing ambitious ownership with passionate fan expectations are not confined to American baseball.

Despite the highly publicized sale of the Dodgers in 2012 and his relocation to new ventures, Frank McCourt maintained a shrewd and ultimately very significant financial connection to the patch of land that had served as the foundation of his Dodgers acquisition: Chavez Ravine. A crucial and often overlooked detail of the intricate 2012 sale agreement was that McCourt strategically retained a 50% ownership stake in the entity that controls the vast Dodger Stadium parking lots. It was the asset he had meticulously carved into Chavez Ravine Properties LLC during his ownership, recognizing its immense, inherent value far beyond its utilitarian function as mere game-day parking. Under the precise terms of the sale agreement with Guggenheim Baseball Management, the new Dodgers owners would, for the foreseeable future, pay an annual lease fee for the perpetual use of these expansive parking facilities. It was not a one-time payment or a short-term arrangement but a binding, long-term commitment that ensured McCourt's continued financial benefit from the stadium he once owned. This lease agreement translates into a substantial passive income stream, estimated at approximately $14 million yearly for Frank McCourt. Every time a car rumbles into one of those sprawling asphalt lots, on every game day that draws tens of thousands of vehicles, a portion of that economic activity quietly funnels directly into

ALLEN SCHERY

McCourt's coffers —a remarkable testament to his financial foresight. This particular arrangement ensures that, even after selling the team for a record-breaking sum and publicly moving on to new, obvious ventures in global sports, Frank McCourt continues to receive a significant, passive, and remarkably consistent income stream directly from the Dodgers' day-to-day operations, year after year, for decades to come. Philosophically, this enduring arrangement highlights the profound and enduring power of his initial, audacious financial engineering; by strategically separating the land from the team's operating assets, he created a perpetual revenue stream for himself, effectively monetizing an integral component of the team's operational existence, even in its post-ownership phase. Psychologically, it speaks volumes about his foresight, meticulous planning, and remarkable ability to secure long-term financial benefits, even in the face of what was, in essence, a forced divestiture, representing a final, ingenious maneuver in his complex and highly successful real estate play. This ongoing financial tether to the Dodgers, although often unpublicized amidst the team's new era of success, serves as a quiet yet powerful reminder of the intricate and pervasive financial web he once wove around the franchise —a financial ghost in the machine, quietly churning out millions annually.

Even after his direct stewardship of the Dodgers concluded, Frank McCourt's influence also extended into ambitious large-scale infrastructure projects within Los Angeles, notably through the active involvement of his son, Drew McCourt, in the proposed Union Station tram project. Drew McCourt, who had served as the Dodgers' executive vice president overseeing ticketing and various business operations during his father's ownership, transitioned into a key role within McCourt Global, the family's diversified investment and development firm, with a focus on large-scale urban development projects. The Union Station tram project, officially known as Aerial Rapid Transit Technologies (ARTT), proposes an innovative aerial gondola system specifically designed to directly connect downtown Los Angeles' historic Union Station, a central public transit hub, with Dodger Stadium. Envision a line of sleek, modern cabins gliding silently above the urban sprawl, offering breathtaking panoramic views of the city skyline and the verdant hills of Elysian Park, whisking fans from the bustling heart of downtown directly to the ballpark gates in a mere seven minutes. This ambitious project, while ostensibly aimed at significantly improving transportation and fan access to the notoriously traffic-choked stadium—a persistent frustration for generations of Dodgers fans—also represented a clear and deliberate continuation of the McCourt family's long-standing interest in leveraging urban real estate and infrastructure for broader economic development and enhanced public access. Drew McCourt's direct involvement in this project, which has inevitably faced various regulatory, environmental, and public acceptance hurdles, particularly from community groups concerned about impacts on local parks and neighborhoods, vividly illustrates the family's continued strategic focus on large-scale urban revitalization and connectivity, especially those initiatives that intersect with existing or future major sports and entertainment venues. As of 2025, the project remains in various stages of environmental review and public approval, still navigating its complex path toward potential realization. The philosophical undercurrent here is the persistent belief in the transformative power of modern infrastructure to unlock latent value in densely populated urban areas, a core tenet that has underpinned much of the McCourt real estate philosophy since their Boston roots. Psychologically, for Drew, leading such a high-profile project, even one tethered to his family's past association with the Dodgers, may represent a significant opportunity to establish his distinct legacy in Los Angeles development, separate from the more controversial aspects that marked his direct tenure with the Dodgers, yet still deeply connected to the city's intricate urban fabric and its most iconic sports venue. The tram project, if it ever secures final approval and navigates its ongoing environmental review processes, would not only address long-standing traffic woes around Dodger Stadium but would also serve as a powerful, tangible symbol of the McCourt family's enduring, albeit now indirect, influence on Los Angeles's dynamic urban landscape.

Meanwhile, Jamie McCourt also embarked on a markedly new and independent chapter following the highly publicized and emotionally draining divorce, meticulously carving out her distinct and influential path in business and politics. After the settlement, which awarded her a significant sum (reportedly around $130 million, providing a substantial capital base for her subsequent endeavors), Jamie strategically pivoted from her previous role as Dodgers CEO into new ventures within the competitive and often cutthroat world of finance and technology. She became a prominent and respected figure in the venture capital world, actively focusing on high-growth technology and life sciences investments, particularly within Silicon Valley's fast-paced and rapidly evolving ecosystem. Notably, she co-founded One World Star Ventures, a venture capital firm investing in early-stage tech companies. Her involvement in various startups, investment funds, and advisory boards demonstrated keen and independent business acumen, separate from the shadow of the Dodgers organization or her former marriage. She became known for her sharp intellect and strategic insights in identifying disruptive technologies and promising new companies, cultivating a network of influential contacts in the tech world. Beyond her burgeoning investment activities, Jamie McCourt also made a notable foray into the diplomatic arena, a stark departure from the highly scrutinized and often combative world of sports business. In 2017, she received an obvious appointment from President Donald Trump as the United States Ambassador to France and Monaco. This prestigious and high-profile diplomatic post required significant experience in international relations, political acumen, and a keen understanding of global affairs. She served in this capacity until January 2021, navigating complex international relations, promoting American interests, and engaging in cultural diplomacy from the elegant U.S. Embassy in Paris. This appointment marked a significant and striking shift into public service and international relations, showcasing a different, multifaceted aspect of her capabilities, ambitions, and public persona. Philosophically, her multifaceted trajectory represents a compelling narrative of profound reinvention, resilience, and personal empowerment, moving definitively beyond the often-negative shadow of a contentious and publicly agonizing divorce to forge a new and respected identity in global finance and high-level diplomacy. Psychologically, her post-Dodgers career reflects a powerful and unyielding drive for independence, public recognition on her terms, and the diligent establishment of her own distinct and positive legacy, entirely separate from the complex and often tumultuous world of professional sports ownership and personal marital disputes. Her successful transition from the highly scrutinized world of sports ownership to influential roles in global finance and international relations serves as a remarkable illustration of her innate capacity for profound adaptation, astute strategic planning, and unwavering continued ambition.

The post-Dodgers lives of Frank, Jamie, and Drew McCourt collectively offer compelling and multifaceted insights into the enduring legacies of their pivotal time with the franchise. For Frank, the strategic acquisition of Olympique Marseille and his continued, quiet financial stake in the revenue-generating Dodger Stadium parking lots underscore a consistent and deeply ingrained philosophical approach: the identification and aggressive leveraging of undervalued assets, whether they be storied sports teams or prime urban real estate, for significant and often perpetual financial gain. Despite the intense public scrutiny and frequently scathing criticism of his tenure with the Dodgers, his remarkable resilience in pursuing new, high-profile ventures speaks to a powerful and seemingly unquenchable psychological drive that remains undiminished by past controversies. For Jamie, her equally impressive journey into venture capital and high-level diplomacy signifies a deliberate and successful move towards establishing an independent identity and global influence, meticulously leveraging her experiences, intellect, and significant financial resources in novel and impactful ways. Drew's continued involvement in the ambitious Union Station tram project, while undeniably linked to the Dodgers' vicinity and its future, suggests a generational continuation of the family's profound interest in large-scale urban real estate and infrastructure development, albeit now with a more explicit focus on public-private partnerships aimed at civic improvement alongside potential profit. The collective narrative of the McCourts after the Dodgers sale is one of dispersal and diversification, yet with undeniable underlying threads of their past strategies, core philosophies, and enduring ambitions. It vividly highlights how the immense capital generated from the record-breaking sale, even under duress, provided the crucial liquidity for genuinely new beginnings, allowing each member to carve out their next significant chapter, forever linked by the dramatic and often tumultuous period they spent at the helm of one of baseball's most iconic franchises, but now pursuing their ambitions on separate, albeit sometimes intersecting, global stages. The complex financial structures, the audacious leveraging of assets, and the unique personal dynamics that so profoundly defined their Dodgers era continue to echo, in various forms, in their subsequent endeavors, demonstrating that while the team itself changed hands, the McCourt family's distinctive entrepreneurial spirit and strategic financial approach found powerful new avenues for expression and substantial profit, even from the very ground they once fully controlled.

Chapter 12
The McCourt Legacy

The tumultuous tenure of Frank McCourt as owner of the Los Angeles Dodgers, spanning from his acquisition in 2004 to his forced divestiture in 2012, remains one of the most controversial and profoundly scrutinized periods in the storied history of the franchise. It was an era marked by audacious financial maneuvers, unprecedented public acrimony, and a dramatic personal unraveling that reverberated through the highest echelons of professional sports. His ownership left an indelible, complex mark on the Dodgers as an institution and the broader baseball industry, prompting a reevaluation of the fundamental principles governing league oversight and franchise stewardship. A reflective examination of McCourt's legacy necessitates a multifaceted approach, delving into how his time is indelibly etched in Dodger history, the critical, hard-won lessons learned by Major League Baseball and its collective owners, and the lasting impact he unwittingly exerted on the intricate, often delicate relationship between sports, finance, and the sacred concept of public trust.

The Indelible Mark on Dodger History

In the cherished annals of Dodger history, Frank McCourt's ownership is overwhelmingly viewed through a lens of profound disappointment, acute embarrassment, and, for countless loyal fans, an almost visceral sense of outright betrayal. The initial wave of boundless optimism that genuinely greeted his arrival in Los Angeles, carefully fueled by his fervent promises of substantial investment in the team and a return to a more "hands-on," community-oriented ownership style, rapidly dissipated. This hopeful sentiment evaporated with alarming speed as his intricate financial strategies became starkly clearer, and his increasingly lavish personal spending habits contrasted with the team's observable parsimony and declining competitive vitality. The psychological impact on the vast and deeply devoted fanbase was devastating and deeply personal. Generations of Dodgers faithful, accustomed to the perceived stability, ethical stewardship, and community-centric approach characteristic of the venerable O'Malley family's long tenure, felt an acute and wrenching sense of alienation as the iconic team they cherished became, in their eyes, a mere pawn in a sprawling, complex financial game and a very public backdrop for a bitter, agonizing personal divorce. His era is predominantly remembered not for on-field championships – despite the occasional flashes of playoff contention – but for the ceaseless off-field drama, the unsettling financial instability that hovered like a dark cloud, and the pervasive, gnawing sense that the team's competitive well-being and long-term vitality were perpetually secondary to the owner's gain and insatiable financial ambitions. The philosophical understanding of a professional sports team as a sacred public trust, deeply embedded in the civic and cultural fabric of Los Angeles, was perceived as fundamentally violated during his tenure, leading to a profound erosion of goodwill and trust that took years for the subsequent ownership group to repair painstakingly. This period is now almost universally cited as a nadir, a stark and enduring reminder of how swiftly and dramatically an iconic, beloved franchise can be destabilized when private financial interests fundamentally clash, often catastrophically, with deeply held public expectations and the inherent civic responsibilities accompanying sports ownership.

A Legacy of Perceived Deception

One of the most enduring, corrosive, and ultimately defining aspects of McCourt's complex legacy is the pervasive and deeply ingrained perception of his dishonesty and systematic deception. This narrative solidified inexorably as his tenure of ownership progressed, and his intricate financial dealings were increasingly and painfully exposed to public scrutiny. A critical and sobering summary of these instances reveals not an isolated error but rather a discernible pattern of misleading public statements and opaque financial practices that relentlessly eroded trust at every conceivable level of his operation:

Misrepresenting Financial Foundation: From the outset, McCourt deliberately presented himself as a cash-rich, financially secure owner, ostensibly capable of infusing significant capital directly into the team and its infrastructure. This foundational claim was later revealed to be profoundly specious, as the rigorous financial disclosures mandated by the divorce proceedings (as meticulously detailed in Chapter 7) unequivocally showed he had put "not a penny" of his liquid cash into the initial $430 million acquisition of the franchise. Instead, he relied entirely on a highly leveraged structure, including a massive $135 million loan directly from the seller, News Corp. This fundamental misrepresentation of his financial foundation —a deliberate obfuscation of his true liquidity —set an early and profoundly disingenuous tone for his entire ownership.

Contradictory Public Statements on Team Finances: He consistently asserted, with unwavering conviction, that the Dodgers were financially sound and fully capable of robustly competing for championships, even as increasingly alarming reports of delayed payments to essential vendors, minor league staff, and even player bonuses began to surface (Chapter 6) surreptitiously. His public rhetoric often painted a meticulously crafted picture of robust fiscal health. This narrative starkly and irreconcilably contradicted the internal financial realities and the mounting, insidious debt later glaringly revealed in publicly accessible court documents. This pervasive duality created a profound and ultimately unbridgeable credibility gap, where his carefully chosen words increasingly diverged from the observable and undeniable facts, leading to a deepening sense of public distrust.

Manipulative Use of Corporate Structures: The meticulous creation of a complex, layered web of corporate entities, most notably the strategic separation of the highly valuable Dodger Stadium parking lots into Chavez Ravine Properties LLC (as explored in Chapter 5), was initially presented by McCourt as a legitimate and forward-thinking strategic business decision primarily aimed at facilitating future development and maximizing overall asset value. However, the subsequent, shocking revelation that the Dodgers were compelled to pay substantial annual "rent"—amounting to approximately $14 million each year—to this McCourt-controlled entity, effectively siphoning cash directly from the team's operational budget into his coffers, was almost universally viewed as a deliberately deceptive maneuver. It was a sophisticated form of financial manipulation thinly disguised as legitimate corporate structuring. It was designed to extract funds for his personal use and the servicing of his burgeoning personal debt rather than for the direct and beneficial investment in the team's competitive needs.

Exploiting Team Assets for Personal Gain: His desperate attempts to secure a massive $3 billion television rights deal with Fox Sports (as detailed in Chapter 8) were publicly presented as the definitive financial lifeline, the ultimate solution to the team's dire economic woes. However, Major League Baseball Commissioner Bud Selig, acting on extensive internal review, unequivocally blocked the deal precisely because a substantial portion of the enormous upfront payment was demonstrably earmarked for McCourt's personal use, including the critical payment of his contentious divorce settlement, rather than being solely dedicated to the team's operational needs or long-term investments. This was an apparent and audacious attempt to leverage a fundamental team asset for overt personal gain under the transparent guise of team solvency —a deceptive act of self-dealing that directly and immediately precipitated MLB's decisive and unprecedented intervention.

Inconsistent Legal Documents: Throughout the intensely public and bitter divorce proceedings, McCourt provided multiple conflicting versions of a crucial post-nuptial agreement (Chapter 7), aggressively attempting to assert sole ownership of the highly valuable Dodgers franchise. The court's eventual and decisive ruling that these varying, inconsistent documents created insurmountable ambiguity and rendered the agreement unenforceable highlighted a deliberate and calculated attempt to mislead the court and manipulate legal outcomes regarding the division of marital assets. It was a direct, undeniable example of legal deception that failed under rigorous judicial scrutiny, further cementing the public's perception of his manipulative tendencies.

Hypocrisy of Personal Spending vs. Team Investment: Finally, the stark, infuriating contrast between his public statements about genuinely investing in the team and the undeniable reality of his extravagant personal spending (as painfully revealed through court documents in Chapter 6) was widely perceived as a profound act of hypocrisy and deep deception. While the team publicly struggled financially, deferring payments and operating on a tight budget, McCourt's seemingly limitless expenditure on multiple luxury homes in exclusive enclaves, private jet travel across continents, and other opulent amenities fueled an overwhelming public outrage and a profound sense of civic betrayal. This stark disparity gave the distinct impression that he was prioritizing his personal, opulent lifestyle over the fundamental competitive needs of the Dodgers, systematically misleading fans about his steadfast commitment to their beloved team.

These numerous instances, collectively and cumulatively, paint a damning picture of an owner whose relationship with objective truth was, at best, fluid and opportunistic and, at worst, deliberately and calculatingly deceptive. This pervasive perception of fundamental dishonesty fundamentally poisoned his relationship with the fanbase, damaged the team's reputation, and ultimately contributed to his inevitable downfall more than any other single factor.

Lessons Learned by Major League Baseball

The lessons learned from the tumultuous McCourt era, particularly by Major League Baseball as a collective entity, were profound, immediate, and far-reaching, fundamentally reshaping the business and governance of professional baseball. The most critical and enduring lesson was the necessity of robust financial vetting and ongoing, vigilant oversight of team ownership. Commissioner Selig's intervention, though unprecedented in its scope and directness, established a powerful and enduring precedent: that the league unequivocally possesses the inherent authority and fundamental responsibility to decisively step in when an owner's financial mismanagement or personal conduct directly threatens the integrity, competitive balance, and long-term stability of a cherished franchise, and by extension, the entire league itself. This profound philosophical shift meticulously reasserted the "best interests of baseball" clause, enshrined in the league's constitution, as a potent and actively wielded regulatory tool. It sent an unmistakable signal that ownership of a Major League Baseball franchise is a privileged stewardship, not an absolute, unfettered right. It inherently comes with a profound implicit social contract with the league and, crucially, with the discerning public. Psychologically, this decisive intervention sent a clear, unambiguous message to all other owners across the league: private property rights, while significant, are ultimately not absolute when their exercise jeopardizes the collective enterprise and the overarching public image of professional baseball. This seminal event led to a significantly more stringent and thorough review process for prospective owners and a much greater emphasis on continuous transparency in team finances, marking a notable departure from previous, more lenient approaches.

Furthermore, the McCourt saga indelibly underscored the critical, indeed existential, importance of systematically separating team finances from an owner's complex personal finances. The intricate web of Limited Liability Companies (LLCs), opaque inter-company loans, and self-serving related-party transactions that McCourt meticulously employed to extract funds from the Dodgers became a quintessential cautionary tale for the entire sports industry. The league and the broader landscape of professional sports taught the severe perils inherent in allowing such indiscriminate commingling, which can obscure proper financial health, create irreconcilable conflicts of interest, and leave a team vulnerable to an owner's liabilities or ambitions. This realization has since led to significantly greater scrutiny of ownership structures across professional sports leagues and a concerted push for clearer, legally enforceable financial boundaries to protect teams from their owners' personal whims, liabilities, or unchecked ambitions. Philosophically, it reinforced the fundamental idea that a sports franchise operates within a unique and obvious public sphere despite being a privately owned business, demanding a higher standard of financial governance, ethical conduct, and transparent accountability than any other private enterprise.

Lasting Impact on the Dodgers and Fanbase

The lasting impact on the Dodgers franchise itself was profound and multifaceted. Initially, the McCourt era regrettably left deep, festering scars: a deeply disillusioned fan base, a financially depleted and almost bankrupt organization, and a severely tarnished reputation that threatened to erode its historical standing permanently. However, the dramatic and ultimately triumphant sale to Guggenheim Baseball Management (as vividly detailed in Chapter 9) and the subsequent ushering in of a "new era" (as explored in Chapter 10) provided an unprecedented opportunity for remarkable healing, profound revitalization, and an inspiring resurgence. The record-breaking sale price of $2.15 billion, while a testament to the Dodgers' undeniable inherent brand value and market potential, also fundamentally reset the benchmarks for franchise valuations across all professional sports, profoundly altering the economics of sports ownership. It compellingly demonstrated that even a team in a state of profound crisis, when armed with a globally recognized brand and operating within a lucrative primary market, could command an astronomical sum, attracting a new breed of ultra-wealthy, globally-minded investors. This phenomenon has contributed significantly to the seemingly relentless inflation of professional sports team values, making ownership an even more exclusive and financially demanding club than ever before.

Psychologically, the Dodgers' fan base underwent a profound and emotionally cathartic transformation. The long years of simmering resentment, deep-seated anger, and gnawing betrayal were gradually, yet systematically, replaced by a renewed sense of unbridled pride, unwavering loyalty, and burgeoning optimism under the new ownership. The visible presence of beloved figures like Magic Johnson and the massive and highly publicized investments in top-tier player talent and critical stadium infrastructure served as a powerful and much-needed antidote to the bitterness of the McCourt years. This process powerfully demonstrated the immense capacity of a loyal fan base to forgive past grievances and enthusiastically re-engage when presented with a palpable, genuine commitment and sustained competitive success. The philosophical lesson for future owners is unequivocally clear: while financial success and profitability are undeniably paramount, they must be meticulously balanced with a profound, empathetic understanding of the team's emotional, cultural, and civic significance. Neglecting or violating this unwritten social contract, as McCourt was widely perceived to do, can lead to devastating and far-reaching consequences for the owner's reputation and legacy, even if they manage to walk away financially enriched.

Frank McCourt's Post-Dodgers Trajectory

Frank McCourt's next chapter, as meticulously explored in Chapter 11, with his strategic acquisition of Olympique Marseille and his continued, consistent income stream from the Dodger Stadium parking lots, serves as a powerful testament to his enduring entrepreneurial spirit and his unwavering, almost instinctive, application of sophisticated leveraging strategies. His son Drew's active involvement in the ambitious Union Station tram project and Jamie's highly successful pivot into the worlds of venture capital and international diplomacy further illustrate the McCourt family's remarkable resilience, continued ambition, and capacity for adaptation, even after a period of intense public scrutiny. However, the shadow of the Dodgers era, particularly the pervasive public perception of his controversial financial dealings and alleged deceptions, remains an undeniable and defining aspect of his complex public persona.

Conclusion: A Cautionary Tale and a Moral Imperative

In conclusion, Frank McCourt's tumultuous ownership of the Los Angeles Dodgers is a compelling and enduring cautionary tale in the modern history of professional sports. It highlighted the inherent vulnerabilities of highly leveraged ownership models, the profound perils of indiscriminately commingling personal and team finances, and the devastating, long-term impact of a perceived fundamental breach of trust with the loyal fan base. Yet, paradoxically, his controversial tenure also inadvertently paved the way for a new, more stringent understanding of league oversight and regulatory authority, fundamentally reasserting the inherent value and public importance of iconic sports brands.

The moral imperative derived from the McCourt saga is clear: While professional sports franchises are undeniably businesses, their profound cultural and civic significance demands a higher ethical standard from their owners. The pursuit of profit, however legitimate, cannot supersede the sacred trust placed in a team's steward by its community. The McCourt legacy is thus a complex, multifaceted mosaic: a period of unprecedented turmoil that ultimately, through a difficult but necessary process, led to a stronger, more financially robust, and profoundly more fan-connected Dodgers franchise, but only after a painful and public reckoning that forever changed the landscape of sports ownership and its underlying responsibilities. The critical lessons gleaned from his tenure continue to resonate, shaping how leagues meticulously vet prospective owners, how teams rigorously manage their complex finances, and how the delicate and essential balance between private enterprise and public trust is continually navigated in the ever-evolving, high-stakes business of professional baseball.

Bibliography

Sources Used

Chapter One

- Next City Staff - "Money Grab" (Article)

- McCormack, Peter - "Real Estate Development Exactions in Boston: Implications for Linkage and Planning In the South Boston Seaport District" (Academic Thesis)

- The McCourt Company (or McCourt Global / McCourt Partners) - "Our History/Timeline" (Website content/company history)

- Forbes Staff - "Who is Frank McCourt, the billionaire trying to buy TikTok?"

- Rich May Law Firm - "John J. Burns" (Firm History/Profile, detailing legal work)

- Boston Magazine Staff - "The Good, the Bad, and the Ugly" (Article)

Chapter Two

- Shaikin, Bob - *Los Angeles Times* (Articles covering the Dodgers' sale process, News Corp.'s divestment, McCourt's bid, and initial financial reports in 2003-2004).

- Shelburne, Ramona - *ESPN.com* (Later, more in-depth investigative pieces and reports, particularly during the McCourt divorce and bankruptcy, which revealed the specific financial mechanisms and leverage of the 2004 acquisition).

- Quinn, T.J. - *ESPN.com* (Similar to Shelburne, contributed to investigative reporting on the financial details of McCourt's ownership, including the original purchase).

- Plaschke, Bill - *Los Angeles Times* (Columns and opinion pieces capturing the initial public and fan reaction in Los Angeles to the new ownership in 2004).

- Simers, T.J. - *Los Angeles Times* (provided critical or cynical commentary)

- **Wetzstein, Cheryl** - *The Washington Times* (Authored specific articles that detailed the terms of the 2004 purchase, including the News Corp. loan, often cited during later legal proceedings).

- **Gelles, Jeff** - *The Philadelphia Inquirer* (reported on the national implications or details of the Dodgers sale).

- **Verducci, Tom** - *Sports Illustrated* (covered major ownership changes and their implications for the league).

- **Fabrikant, Geraldine** - *The New York Times* (covered deal involving News Corp.).

- **Bud Selig (then MLB Commissioner)** - (Official statements or interviews regarding the approval of McCourt's ownership).

Chapter Three

- **Plaschke, Bill** - *Los Angeles Times* (Numerous columns and reports from 2004-2007 on McCourt's early ownership, fan reaction, stadium improvements, player personnel decisions, and ticketing issues).

- **Shaikin, Bob** - *Los Angeles Times* (Various articles covering the business aspects of McCourt's early tenure, stadium plans and costs, payroll details, and operational decisions).

- Simers, T.J. - *Los Angeles Times* (Various columns offering often critical and cynical perspectives on McCourt's business practices, perceived miserliness, and their impact on the team and fans during the early years).

- Wharton, David - *Los Angeles Times* (Articles focusing on the Dodgers' business operations, including stadium developments and ticketing strategies).

- Wetzstein, Cheryl - *The Washington Times* (Various articles)

- McCourt, Frank H. Jr. - Public statements, press conference transcripts, and interviews from 2004-2007 detailing his initial vision, promises for investment, and responses to public criticism.

Chapter Four

- Plaschke, Bill - *Los Angeles Times* (Numerous columns and reports from 2004-2011 on Dodgers' playoff runs, key player performances, management changes, and the persistent fan frustration regarding McCourt's financial approach).

- **Shaikin, Bob** - *Los Angeles Times* (Various articles covering the Dodgers' business operations, team payrolls, financial decisions affecting player acquisitions and retention, and the intertwining of McCourt's personal finances with team spending).

- **Shelburne, Ramona** - *ESPN.com* (Many articles and analyses on the McCourt era, detailing on-field performance in the context of ownership's financial pressures, player reactions, and the impact of key figures like Manny Ramirez).

- **Simers, T.J.** - *Los Angeles Times* Various columns offering often pointed critiques of the McCourt ownership, linking team performance, player decisions, and perceived lack of investment to the owner's broader financial strategies).

- **Gurnick, Ken** - *MLB.com* (Official team reporter, would have covered daily game reports, major player transactions, managerial changes, and team progress throughout the 2004-2011 seasons).

- **Ortiz, Jose Luis** - *USA Today* (Articles contrasting Dodgers' spending with other large-market teams, and general baseball financial trends during the McCourt years).

- Verducci, Tom - *Sports Illustrated* (Feature articles and analysis on key players, managerial tenures, and the overall competitive landscape of the Dodgers under McCourt).

- Joe Torre / Don Mattingly - (Books, interviews, or public statements by former managers reflecting on their tenures, the team's dynamics, and the environment under McCourt's ownership).

Chapter Five

- Plaschke, Bill - *Los Angeles Times* (Numerous columns chronicling the mounting public frustration with McCourt's ownership, particularly concerning the financial aspects and perceived lack of investment in the team).

- Shaikin, Bob - *Los Angeles Times* (Extensive reporting on the Dodgers' financial labyrinth, including articles detailing the leveraging of the parking lots, the complex corporate structures, and the flow of money within McCourt's entities).

- Shelburne, Ramona - *ESPN.com* (Deep dive investigative pieces, particularly from later in McCourt's tenure, that meticulously unraveled the financial transactions, the separation of assets, related-party dealings, and the ensuing legal battles).

- Simers, T.J. - *Los Angeles Times* (Various Columns often highlighting the perceived personal enrichment of McCourt at the expense of the team, and the operational flaws under his management).

- Wharton, David - *Los Angeles Times* (Various articles focusing on the real estate aspects of McCourt's ownership, potential development plans for Chavez Ravine, and the valuation of the Dodgers' physical assets).

Chapter Six

- Plaschke, Bill - *Los Angeles Times* (Numerous columns and reports from the mid-to-late 2000s, vividly capturing the mounting fan frustration, perceived financial neglect, and the clash between McCourt's image and reality).

- Shikin, Bob - *Los Angeles Times* (Extensive investigative reporting detailing the Dodgers' financial health, reports of delayed payments, the use of team revenue for personal expenses, and the complexities of McCourt's corporate structure).

- Shelburne, Ramona - *ESPN.com* (In-depth investigative pieces and analyses, particularly those that meticulously uncovered the financial details of McCourt's personal spending and the impact on team operations and public perception).

- Wharton, David - *Los Angeles Times* (Articles focusing on the intersection of the Dodgers' real estate assets, financial valuations, and McCourt's personal financial dealings as they became increasingly public).

- Simers, T.J. - *Los Angeles Times* (Various columns often critical of McCourt's leadership, linking the team's perceived financial issues to the owner's personal wealth and the declining fan morale).

- Bloomberg Businessweek Staff - (Reports on sports ownership models and the financial challenges faced by high-profile sports franchises during this period, often citing the Dodgers as a case study).

- McCourt, Frank H. Jr. / Jamie McCourt - (Public statements, press conference transcripts, and, as they became publicly accessible, excerpts from court depositions during the divorce proceedings that revealed details of their finances and the team's financial state).

- Fan Blogs & Forums (e.g., DodgerBlues.com, True Blue LA, independently organized fan protest sites) - (While not academic sources, these offer crucial insights into the real-time sentiment, organized efforts, and expressions of discontent among the fanbase during this period. Used primarily for understanding psychological impact and sentiment, to be corroborated by media reports).

Chapter Seven

- Plaschke, Bill - *Los Angeles Times* (Numerous columns expressing public and fan outrage over the divorce, its impact on the team, and the financial disclosures made in court).

- Wharton, David - *Los Angeles Times* (Various articles focusing on the financial aspects of divorce, particularly how it exposed the leveraging of team assets and the complex corporate structure).

- Jamie McCourt - (Public statements, legal filings, and interviews given during and after the divorce proceedings, providing her perspective and detailing her claims).

- Frank McCourt - (Public statements, legal filings, and interviews providing his counterarguments and explanations during the divorce and MLB intervention).

- Court Transcripts and Filings - (While not listing specific documents, the extensive media reporting would be based on access to these public records, which detailed financial accounts, sworn testimonies, and legal arguments).

- Bud Selig (MLB Commissioner) - (Public statements, press conference transcripts, and later published accounts or interviews detailing MLB's growing concerns and the justification for the league's intervention in the Dodgers' affairs).

Chapter Eight

- Shelburne, Ramona - *ESPN.com* (Extensive and pivotal reporting during the entire MLB intervention, providing minute-by-minute updates on the legal battles, financial revelations, and the bidding process for the team).

- **Shaikin, Bob** - *Los Angeles Times* (Comprehensive coverage of MLB's takeover, the court proceedings between McCourt and the league, and the eventual sale process and its financial details).

- **Plaschke, Bill** - *Los Angeles Times* (Numerous columns reflecting fan sentiment, the impact of the ownership crisis on the team, and reactions to Selig's intervention and the ultimate sale).

- **Wharton, David** - *Los Angeles Times* (Reporting focused on the financial aspects of the MLB takeover, McCourt's efforts to refinance, the value of the team's assets, and the record-breaking sale price).

- **Selig, Bud** - (Public statements, press conference transcripts, and interviews given during and after the intervention, explaining his decisions and the league's rationale).

- **Tom Schieffer** - (Public statements and reports from the independent monitor during his oversight of the Dodgers' operations).

- McCourt, Frank H. Jr. - (Legal filings, public statements, and interviews detailing his legal challenges to MLB's authority and his attempts to maintain ownership).

- Baseball America Staff - (Various articles providing insights into the baseball operations perspective of the instability and the hopes for new ownership).

- Guggenheim Baseball Management (Mark Walter, Stan Kasten, Magic Johnson) - (Public statements and interviews from the new ownership group following their acquisition of the Dodgers).

Chapter Nine

- Shelburne, Ramona - *ESPN.com* (Extensive and pivotal reporting on the bidding process, the various contenders, the motivations behind the high valuations, and the details of the final sale agreement).

- Shaikin, Bob - *Los Angeles Times* (Comprehensive coverage of the sale process, including the involvement of financial advisors, the legal aspects of the transfer, and the allocation of the sale proceeds).

- **Plaschke, Bill** - *Los Angeles Times* (Numerous columns capturing the palpable sense of relief and celebration among the fanbase, the symbolic importance of the new ownership, and the high hopes for the franchise's future).

- **Wharton, David** - *Los Angeles Times* (Focused reporting on the financial aspects of the sale, including the specific figures for the bid, the underlying asset valuations like real estate and media rights, and the complex financial unwinding for Frank McCourt).

- **Selig, Bud** - (Public statements and press conference transcripts surrounding the conclusion of the sale, expressing the league's satisfaction and vision for the Dodgers' future).

- **Guggenheim Baseball Management (Mark Walter, Stan Kasten, Earvin "Magic" Johnson)** - (Public statements, press conferences, and interviews from the new ownership group, outlining their vision for the team, their commitment to the community, and their plans for baseball operations).

- Frank McCourt - (Public statements or legal representatives' comments following the sale, addressing the outcome and the resolution of his financial obligations).

- Investment Banking Firms / Financial Advisors - (Public reports or statements from the firms involved in managing the sale process, such as Blackstone Group, detailing the methodology and outcome of the auction).

Chapter Ten

- Shelburne, Ramona - *ESPN.com* (Extensive reporting on the Guggenheim group's acquisition, their immediate actions, key trades like the Boston blockbuster, and their commitment to community engagement).

- Shaikin, Bob - *Los Angeles Times* (Comprehensive coverage of the new ownership's financial investments, stadium improvements, and the return to aggressive player acquisition).

- Plaschke, Bill - *Los Angeles Times* (Numerous columns chronicling the renewed optimism among the fanbase, the impact of Magic Johnson's involvement, and the team's return to competitive relevance).

- **Wharton, David** - *Los Angeles Times* (Articles focusing on the financial strategies of the new ownership, the new television deal, and the long-term economic outlook for the franchise).

- **Guggenheim Baseball Management (Mark Walter, Stan Kasten, Earvin "Magic" Johnson)** - (Public statements, press conferences, and interviews outlining their vision, philosophy, and specific actions taken to revitalize the team and reconnect with the community).

- **Mattingly, Don** - (Interviews or statements from the Dodgers manager reflecting on the change in ownership and its impact on the team's morale and competitive approach).

- **Kershaw, Clayton** - (Player interviews reflecting on the changes in team investment and the renewed commitment to winning under the new ownership).

Chapter Eleven

- **Shaikin, Bob** - *Los Angeles Times* (Reporting on the complex financial aspects of the Dodgers sale, specifically detailing the retention of the parking lot ownership and its financial terms).

- Shelburne, Ramona - *ESPN.com* (Analysis and reports on Frank McCourt's post-Dodgers ventures, particularly his move into European football ownership and the ongoing financial connections to the Dodgers).

- Wharton, David - *Los Angeles Times* (Articles focusing on the long-term financial implications of the Dodgers sale, including McCourt's continued income streams from the parking lots and the broader context of his real estate strategy).

- L'Équipe Staff / Le Monde Staff (French media outlets that extensively covered Frank McCourt's acquisition and subsequent management of Olympique Marseille).

- Politi, Daniel - *Los Angeles Times* (Reporting on the Union Station Aerial Tram project, including details about its development, community engagement, and Drew McCourt's involvement).

- Government Records / State Department Announcements - (Official public records confirming Jamie McCourt's ambassadorial appointment and tenure).

- Venture Capital / Tech Publications - (Articles and interviews with Jamie McCourt regarding investment strategies and involvement in the technology and life sciences sectors).

- McCourt, Frank H. Jr. - (Public statements and interviews regarding his acquisition and plans for Olympique Marseille).

- McCourt, Jamie - (Interviews and statements regarding her career in venture capital and her diplomatic role as Ambassador).

- McCourt, Drew - (Public statements or interviews regarding his involvement in McCourt Global and the Union Station tram project).

Chapter Twelve

- **Since this is a summary chapter all the above apply**